Dragons and Other Fantastic Creatures in origami

Other books by John Montroll
www.johnmontroll.com

General Origami

Origami Worldwide
Teach Yourself Origami: Second Revised Edition
Christmas Origami
Storytime Origami

Animal Origami

Bugs in Origami
Horses in Origami
Origami Birds
Origami Gone Wild
Dinosaur Origami
Origami Dinosaurs for Beginners
Mythological Creatures and the Chinese Zodiac Origami
Origami Under the Sea
Sea Creatures in Origami
Origami for the Enthusiast
Animal Origami for the Enthusiast

Geometric Origami

Origami and Math: Simple to Complex
Classic Polyhedra Origami
A Constellation of Origami Polyhedra

Dollar Bill Origami

Dollar Bill Animals in Origami
Dollar Bill Origami
Easy Dollar Bill Origami

Simple Origami

Fun and Simple Origami: 101 Easy-to-Fold Projects
Super Simple Origami
Easy Dollar Bill Origami
Easy Origami

Dragons and Other Fantastic Creatures in origami

JOHN MONTROLL

Dover Publications, Inc.
New York

To Charley and Glenn

Bibliographical Note

Dragons and Other Fantastic Creatures in Origami is a new work,
first published by Dover Publications, Inc., in 2014.

Library of Congress Cataloging-in-Publication Data

Montroll, John.
 Dragons and other fantastic creatures in origami / John Montroll.
   pages cm
 Summary: "Instructions for 27 models of fantasy figures including 10 dragons, a wizard,
ogre, unicorn, phoenix, and other imaginary creatures"– Provided by publisher.
 ISBN 978-0-486-49466-1 (paperback)
 1. Origami. 2. Dragons–Miscellanea. I. Title.
 TT872.5.M64895 2014
 736'.982–dc23   2014
                                                                                        2013048214

Manufactured in the United States by Courier Corporation
49466701   2014
www.doverpublications.com

Introduction

ome join this grand adventure into the realm of the Enchanted Forest. Dragons and other fantastic creatures await you as you journey through this magical land, full of perils and great rewards.

In the Dragon's Lair, you will encounter ten dragons, each with their own challenges and rewards. Along the way you will meet four humanoid creatures and nine fantastic creatures. Useful information about each creature will lead you to success. Once you have captured all the creatures, you will become the Enchanted Master of Origami. Prepare yourself by folding the Enchanted Armament for protection.

The dragons include one, two, and three-headed versions, some featuring differing head details. The humanoids include a Wizard, Ogre, and some Martians. Fantastic creatures include such favorites as Pegasus, a Unicorn, Winged Lion, and a Wyvern. The models range from simple to very complex. Each model is folded from one square sheet of paper, and a story line with photos of each model keeps the reading and folding experience enjoyable.

Along with the magic of the Enchanted Forest, I hope you will also appreciate the magic of origami. Many new origami bases, structures, and techniques have been developed for these models. I strive to keep the models fun to fold, with elegance and efficiency in the folding structure. The finished models feature fine details with clean lines, and hold without spreading or use of tape, and the models are arranged to allow you to improve your origami skills. I hope these models inspire you to continue with many other origami animals.

The diagrams are drawn in the internationally approved Randlett-Yoshizawa style, which is easy to follow once you have learned the basic folds. You can use any kind of square paper for these models, but the best results can be achieved using standard origami paper, which is colored on one side and white on the other. In these diagrams, shading represents the colored side. Large sheets are easier to use than small ones. Origami supplies can be found in arts and craft shops, or at Dover Publications online: www.doverpublications.com. You can also visit OrigamiUSA at www.origamiusa.org for origami supplies and other related information including an extensive list of local, national, and international origami groups.

Many people helped to make this book possible. I thank Constantin Miranda for photographing several models. I thank my editor, Charley Montroll. I also thank the many folders who proofread the diagrams.

John Montroll

www.johnmontroll.com

Contents

★   Simple
★★   Intermediate
★★★   Complex
★★★★   Very Complex

Enchanted Armament

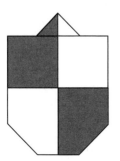

Shield 14
★

Sword 16
★★

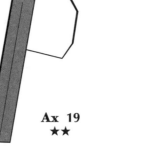

Ax 19
★★

Staff 21
★★

Dragon's Lair

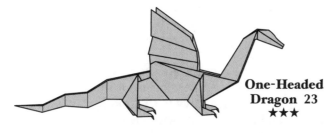

**One-Headed
Dragon 23**
★★★

**Two-Headed
Dragon 28**
★★★

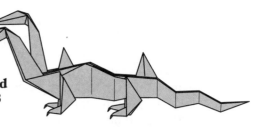

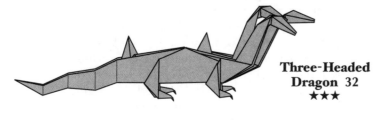

**Three-Headed
Dragon 32**
★★★

**Medieval
Dragon 37**
★★★

Dragon with Claws 41
★★★

Standing Dragon 46
★★★

Chinese Dragon 51
★★★

Western Dragon 56
★★★

Western Dragon with Horns 61
★★★

**Three-Headed
Standing Dragon 66**
★★★

Friend or Foe

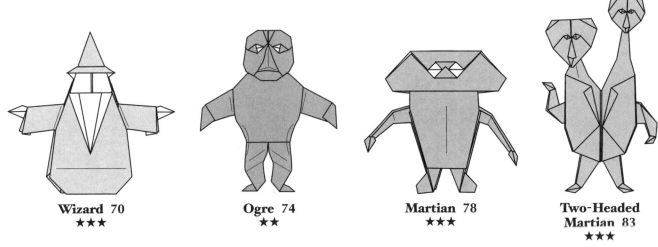

Fantastic Creatures

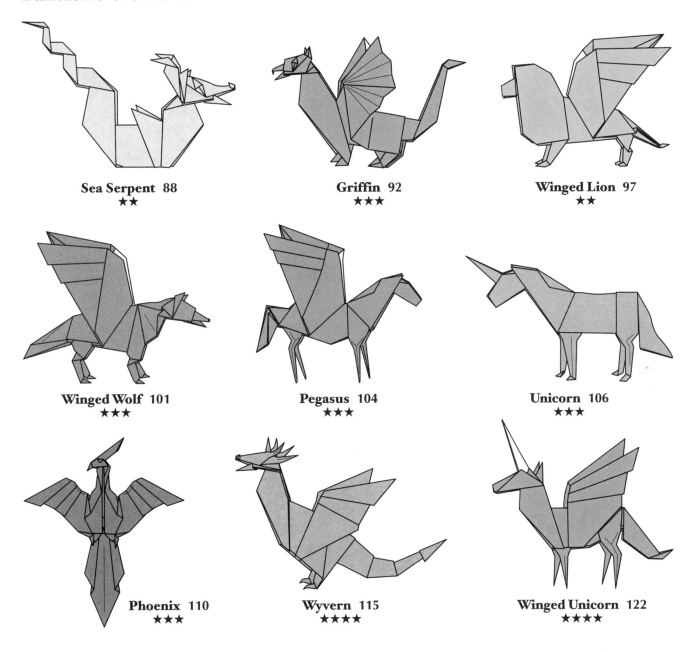

Symbols

Lines

— — — — — — — —   Valley fold, fold in front.

— ·· — · — ·· — · — ··   Mountain fold, fold behind.

_____   Crease line.

....   X-ray or guide line.

Arrows

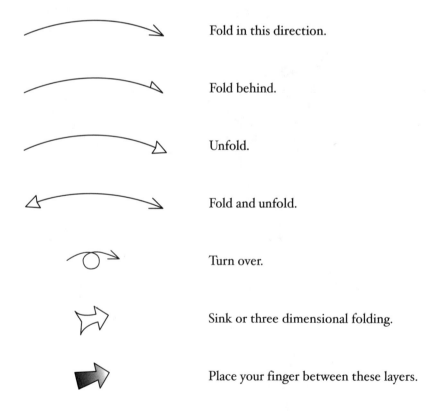

Fold in this direction.

Fold behind.

Unfold.

Fold and unfold.

Turn over.

Sink or three dimensional folding.

Place your finger between these layers.

Basic Folds

Pleat Fold.

Fold back and forth. Each pleat is composed of one valley and mountain fold. Here are two examples.

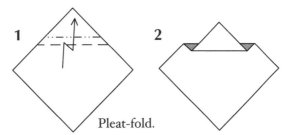

Pleat-fold.

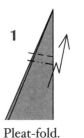

Pleat-fold.

Squash Fold.

In a squash fold, some paper is opened and then made flat. The shaded arrow shows where to place your finger.

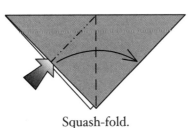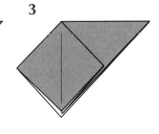

Squash-fold.　　A 3D step.

Petal Fold.

In a petal fold, one point is folded up while two opposite sides meet each other.

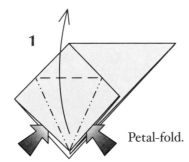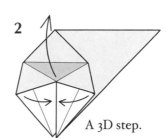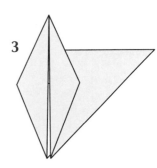

Petal-fold.　　A 3D step.

Rabbit Ear.

To fold a rabbit ear, one corner is folded in half and laid down to a side.

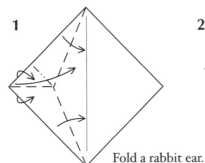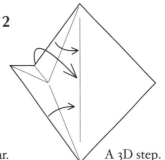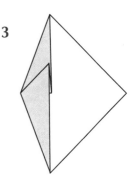

Fold a rabbit ear.　　A 3D step.

Double Rabbit Ear.

If you were to bend a straw you would be folding the double rabbit ear.

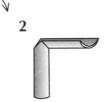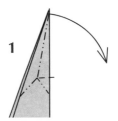

(Straw)　　Double-rabbit-ear.

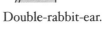

Inside Reverse Fold.

In an inside reverse fold, some paper is folded between layers. Here are two examples.

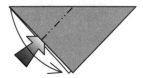

Reverse-fold.

Reverse-fold.

Outside Reverse Fold.

Much of the paper must be unfolded to make an outside reverse fold.

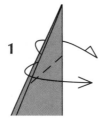

Outside-reverse-fold.

Crimp Fold.

A crimp fold is a combination of two reverse folds. Open the model slightly to form the crimp evenly on each side. Here are two examples.

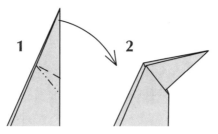

Crimp-fold.

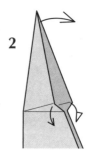

Crimp-fold.   A 3D step.

Sink.

For a sink, some of the paper without edges is folded inside. To do this fold, much of the model must be unfolded.

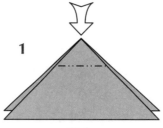

Sink.

Spread Squash Fold.

A cross between a squash fold and sink fold, some paper in the center is spread apart and then made flat.

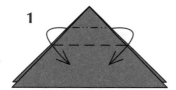

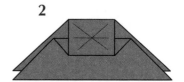

Spread-squash-fold.

10   *Dragons and Other Fantastic Creatures in Origami*

Preliminary Fold.

The Preliminary Fold is the starting point for many models. The maneuver in step 3 occurs in many other models.

1

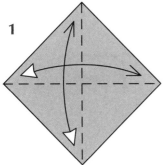

Fold and unfold.

2

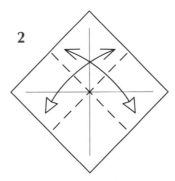

Fold and unfold.

3

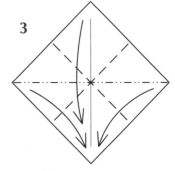

Collapse the square by bringing the four corners together.

4

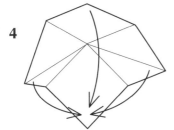

This is 3D.

5

Preliminary Fold

Bird Base.

Historically, the Bird Base has been a very popular starting point. The folds used in it occur in many models.

1

Begin with the Preliminary Fold. Kite-fold, repeat behind.

2

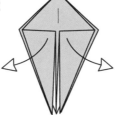

Unfold, repeat behind.

3

Repeat behind.

4

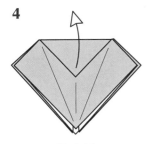

Unfold.

5

Petal-fold, repeat behind.

6

Repeat behind.

7

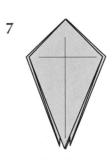

Bird Base

Blintz Frog Base.

This uses the double unwrap fold which is shown in detail below.

1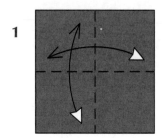

Fold and unfold.

2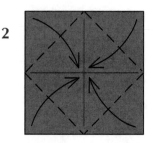

Blintz fold: Fold the four corners to the center.

3

4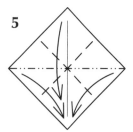

Fold and unfold.

5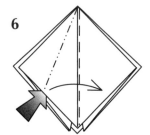

This is similar to the Preliminary Fold.

6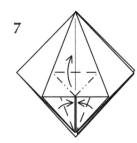

(Diagram enlarged.) Squash-fold.

7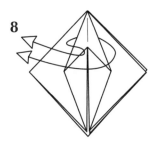

Petal-fold.

8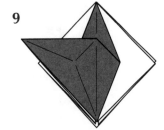

Double-unwrap-fold.

9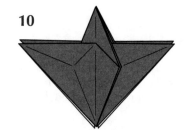

Repeat steps 6–8 three more times, on the back and sides.

10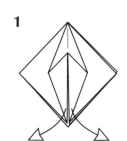

Blintz Frog Base

Double Unwrap Fold.

In the double unwrap fold, locked layers are unwrapped and refolded. Much of the folding is 3D. The diagrams are depicted as shown in steps 8 and 9 of the Blintz Frog Base.

1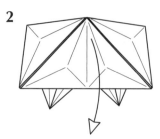

Begin with step 8 of the Blintz Frog Base. Spread at the bottom.

2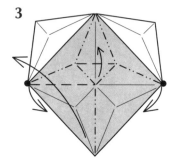

Unfold the top layer.

3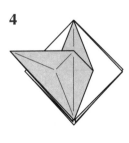

Refold along the creases. The dots will meet at the bottom.

4

12 *Dragons and Other Fantastic Creatures in Origami*

Appreciating Fantastic Creatures

People have been fascinated by dragons for thousands of years. In modern times, dragons are found in blockbuster movies, fantasy novels, and even a popular Children's song. There must be some reason for the longevity of the dragon throughout history, and perhaps there is a kernel of truth to the stories that have been told through the ages.

When humans were the new species on the planet, they were chased and surrounded by all manner of scary creatures, and throughout the millennia have adapted to their surroundings. Imagine turning around and seeing a huge animal hovering over you, its hot breath blowing on your neck; it might not have been an actual flame, but to early Man, it must have felt like fire. Think of all the huge lizards that roamed, and still roam the Earth, add some scary shadows, and you have a dragon. There is no limit to the imagination when one is faced with something they cannot understand.

Early cultures took all of these experiences and created stories from them, stories that might teach, warn and even entertain, and passed them on from shaman to village, and

as the written word became known, these stories that had been passed down through generations became the myths, or perhaps the explanations, of how life worked. A story of a kindly dragon might serve as an example of how a person could make friends with someone they feared, and a person could learn bravery and cunning by hearing a story about how a brave knight outwitted a Three-Headed Dragon.

In addition to dragons, there have been other mythical creatures that have also captured our imaginations. Often these creatures consisted of different parts of several animals known for their strength, wisdom, and other abilities. It was thought that by revering these creatures, we, too, would gain their abilities, be they power, riches, or love.

No matter what time period we are in, there will always be stories of dragons and other powerful creatures. While some fear dragons, still many more see dragons as representing fears and failures they wish to surmount; the difference vanquishing your own dragon can make in your own life makes one wonder if dragons aren't so bad to have around after all?

❊ Enchanted Armament ❊

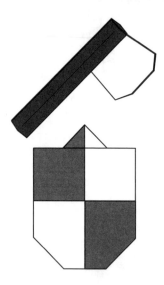

Welcome to the Enchanted Forest, home to dragons and other fantastic creatures. As you begin your adventure on the outskirts of the Forest, be prepared to meet friend and foe alike. In this Forest, you will find both glory and danger, and to keep you safe from harm, you will need your sword and shield, ax and staff. These tools will protect you and aid you in capturing the magic creatures, one by one, that live there. Your powers will grow with every creature you best, but know this: you will not be able to leave the Enchanted Forest until you have captured and tamed them all. Should you survive these trials, you will be crowned Enchanted Master of Origami!

Enter at your peril.

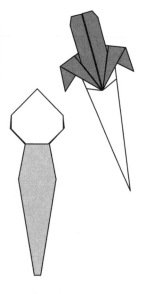

Shield

Danger awaits! To enter the Dragon's Lair and the places beyond, you must have the protection of the shield. Choose your colors wisely, mixing the wrong color with the wrong beast will not end well. Once you have the power of the shield, you can proceed with caution.

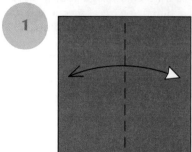

1

Fold and unfold.

2

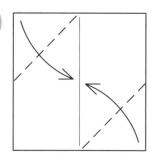

3

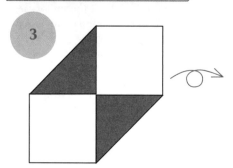

4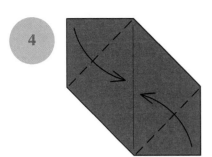

5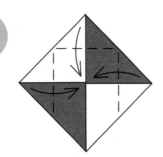

Bring three corners to the center.

6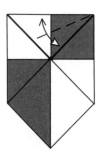

Fold and unfold the top flap.

7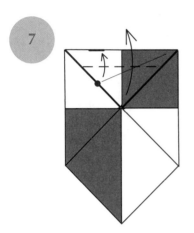

8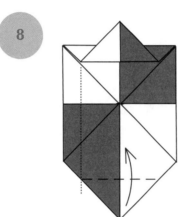

The exact location of the fold is not important.

9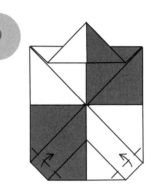

10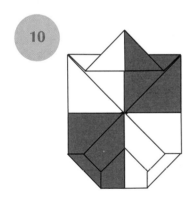

11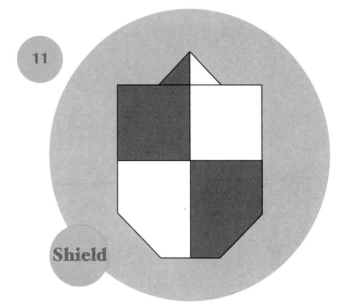

Shield

Shield 15

Sword

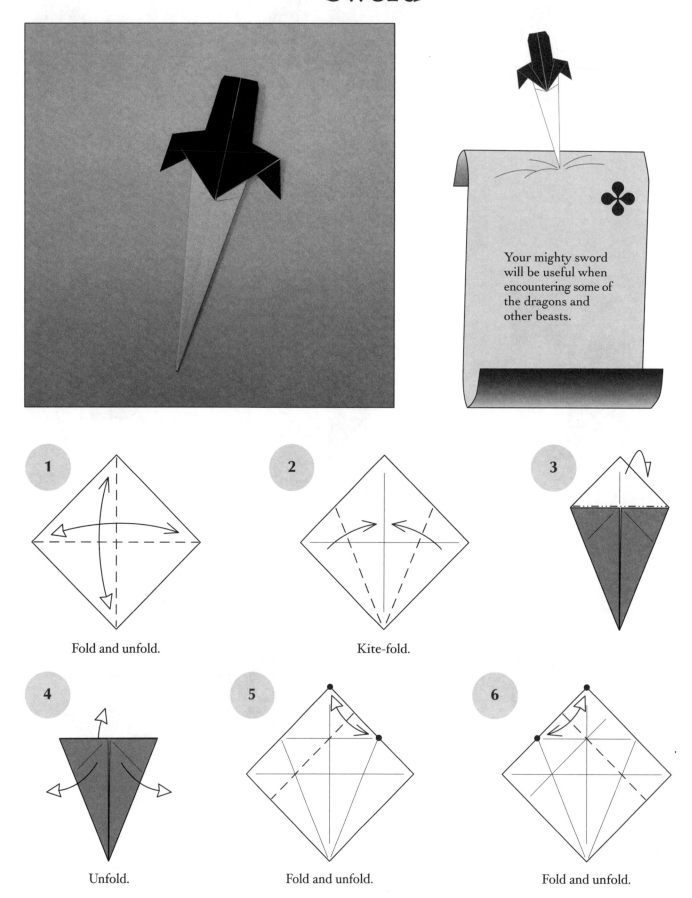

Your mighty sword will be useful when encountering some of the dragons and other beasts.

1 Fold and unfold.

2 Kite-fold.

3

4 Unfold.

5 Fold and unfold.

6 Fold and unfold.

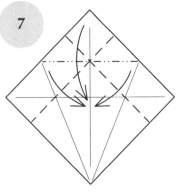

7

This is similar to the preliminary fold.

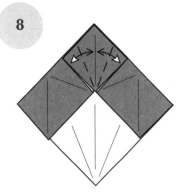

8

Fold and unfold.

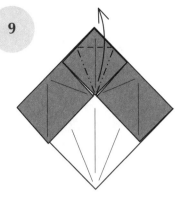

9

Petal-fold.

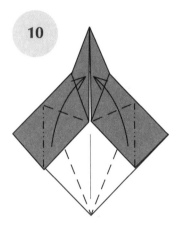

10

Squash folds.

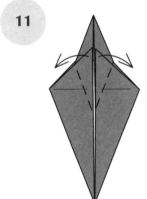

11

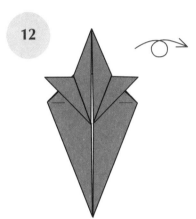

12

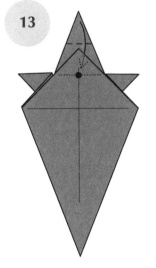

13

Tuck inside.

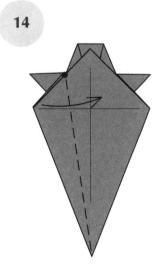

14

Fold past the center.

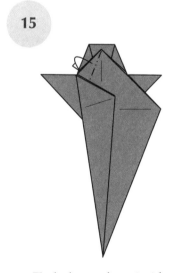

15

Tuck the top layer inside.

Sword 17

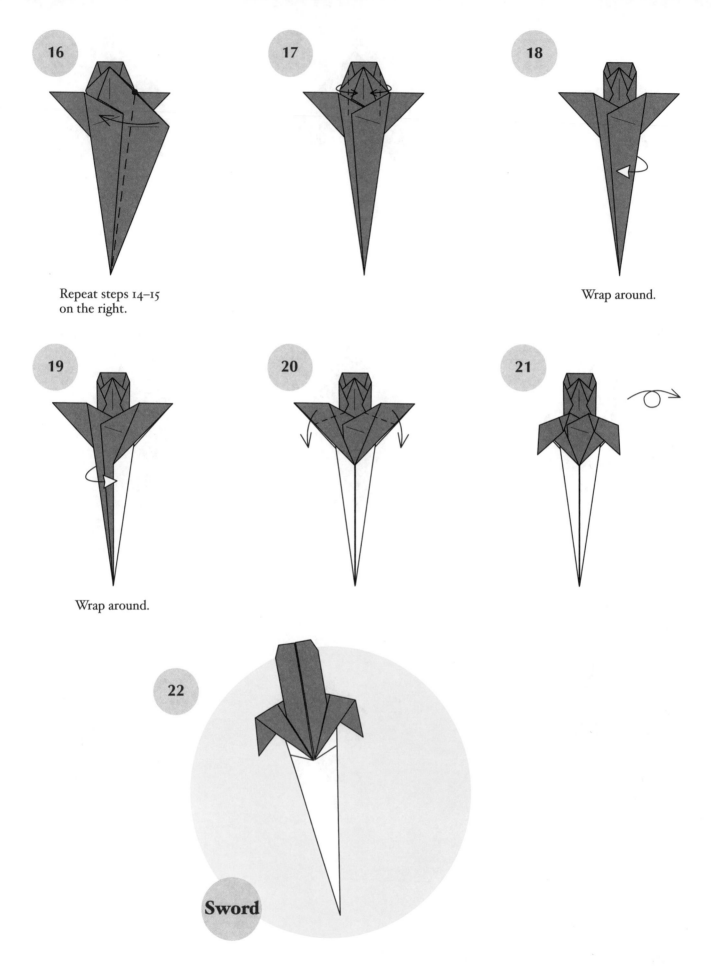

16

Repeat steps 14–15
on the right.

17

18

Wrap around.

19

Wrap around.

20

21

22

Sword

Ax

The ax will be necessary when encountering some of the beasts. Yet it might also be dangerous if it falls in the claws of the wrong creature. Use your ax wisely.

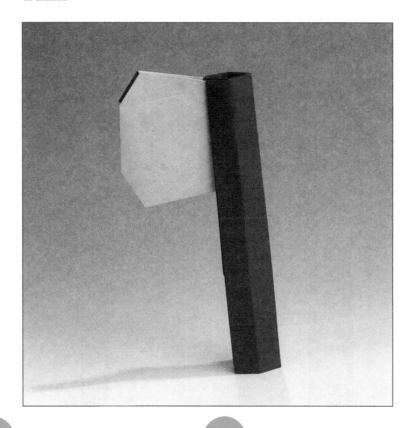

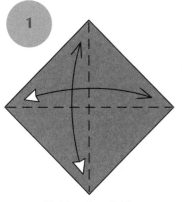

Fold and unfold.

Kite-fold and unfold.

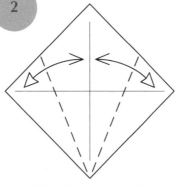

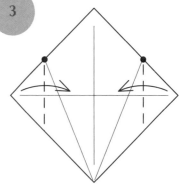

Fold to the center.

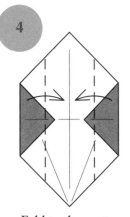

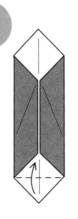

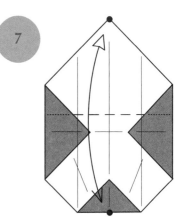

Unfold.

Fold and unfold
in the center.

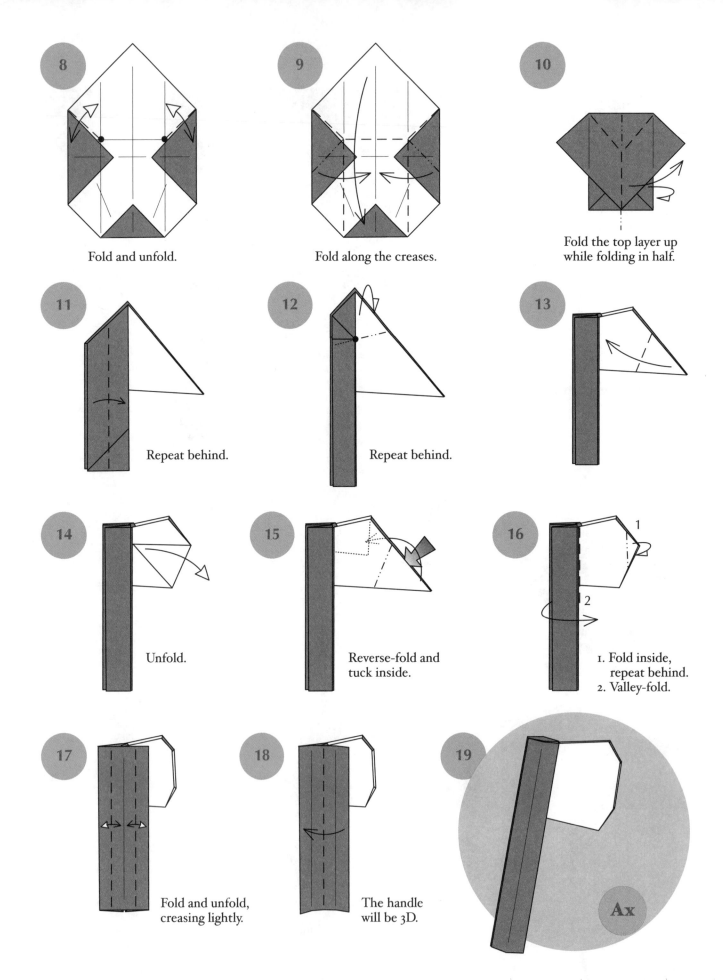

8 Fold and unfold.

9 Fold along the creases.

10 Fold the top layer up while folding in half.

11 Repeat behind.

12 Repeat behind.

13

14 Unfold.

15 Reverse-fold and tuck inside.

16 1. Fold inside, repeat behind. 2. Valley-fold.

17 Fold and unfold, creasing lightly.

18 The handle will be 3D.

19 Ax

20 *Dragons and Other Fantastic Creatures in Origami*

Staff

The staff will give you magical powers. When you first acquire the staff, you will have the power of light, useful when entering dark caves. By capturing each beast, your staff will become progressively more powerful.

1

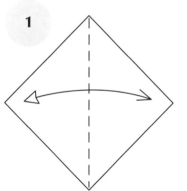

Fold and unfold.

2

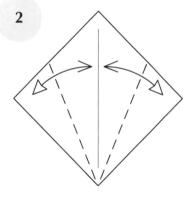

Kite-fold and unfold.

3

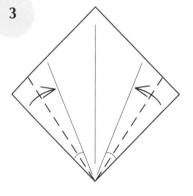

4

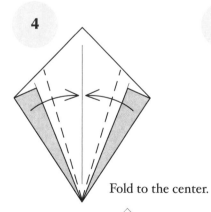

Fold to the center.

5

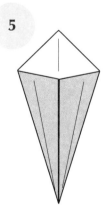

6

7

Fold to the center.

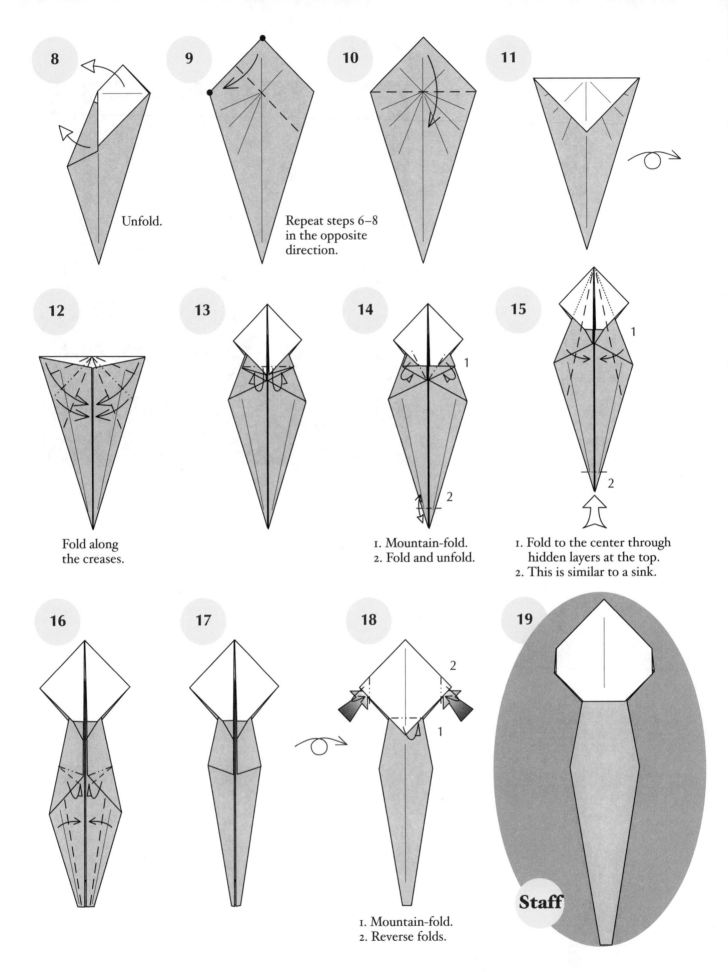

8

Unfold.

9

Repeat steps 6–8
in the opposite
direction.

10

11

12

Fold along
the creases.

13

14

1. Mountain-fold.
2. Fold and unfold.

15

1. Fold to the center through
hidden layers at the top.
2. This is similar to a sink.

16

17

18

1. Mountain-fold.
2. Reverse folds.

19

Staff

❉ Dragon's Lair ❉

Welcome to the Dragon's Lair, home to ten dragon varieties. For centuries, cultures around the world imagined these monsters as huge fire-breathing reptiles, most bearing wings, scales, and claws. Within this lair, you will encounter many of these dragons with different numbers of heads and varied dispositions. Enter with your Enchanted Armament, and be brave and smart as you set out to capture and tame each fire-breathing creature and become the Master of the Enchanted Dragons.

One-Headed Dragon

The One-Headed Dragon feeds on birds and small mammals. It can sense danger from far away. Should it notice you nearby with a sword or ax, the dragon will fly away.

Approach this creature with your shield and staff. Offer your staff and the dragon will be your friend. It will then return your staff, you will now have the power to call upon this creature to come to your side at any time.

1

Fold and unfold.

2

Fold to the center.

3

Kite-fold.

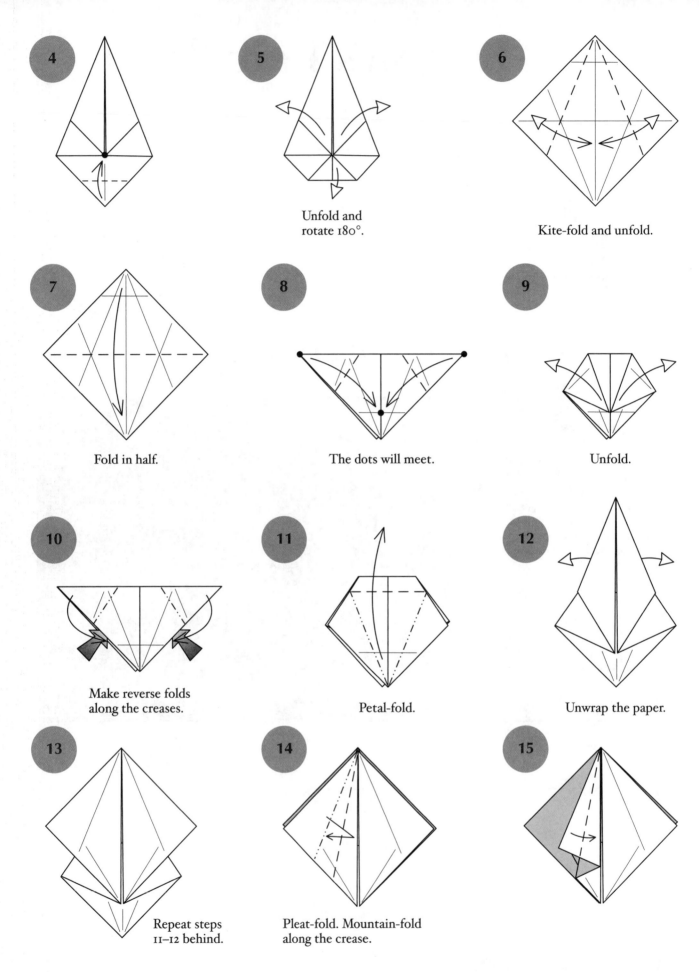

4

5

Unfold and
rotate 180°.

6

Kite-fold and unfold.

7

Fold in half.

8

The dots will meet.

9

Unfold.

10

Make reverse folds
along the creases.

11

Petal-fold.

12

Unwrap the paper.

13

Repeat steps
11–12 behind.

14

Pleat-fold. Mountain-fold
along the crease.

15

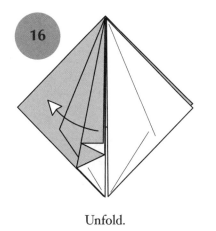

16

Unfold.

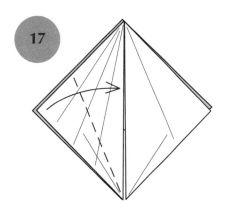

17

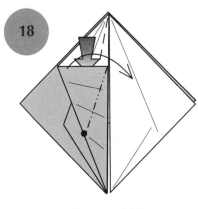

18

Reverse-fold.

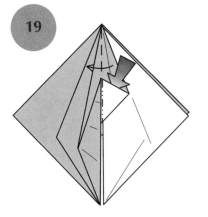

19

Reverse-fold.

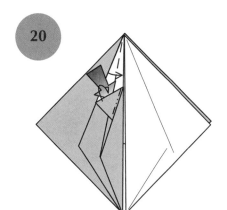

20

Reverse-fold.

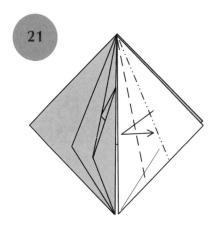

21

Repeat steps 14–20
on the right.

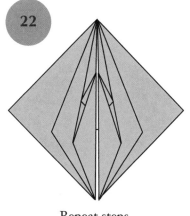

22

Repeat steps
14–21 behind.

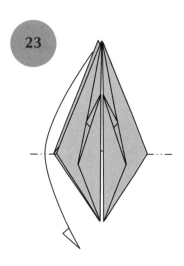

23

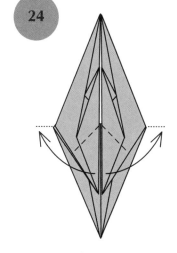

24

Fold to the
dotted lines.

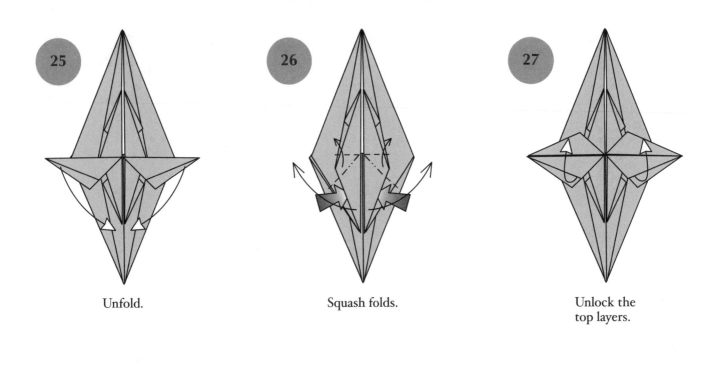

25 Unfold.

26 Squash folds.

27 Unlock the top layers.

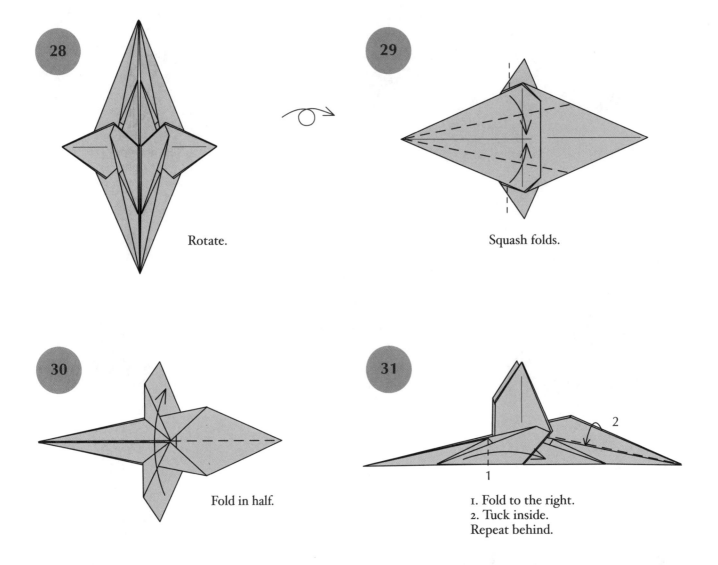

28 Rotate.

29 Squash folds.

30 Fold in half.

31
1. Fold to the right.
2. Tuck inside.
Repeat behind.

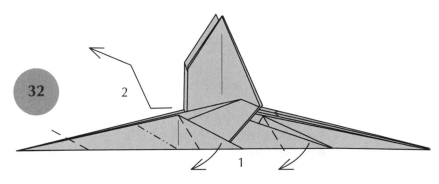

32

1. Fold the legs, repeat behind.
2. Reverse folds.

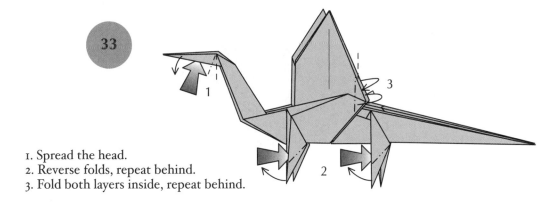

33

1. Spread the head.
2. Reverse folds, repeat behind.
3. Fold both layers inside, repeat behind.

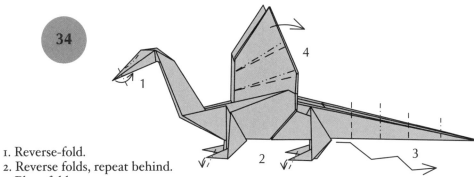

34

1. Reverse-fold.
2. Reverse folds, repeat behind.
3. Pleat-fold.
4. Pleat-fold, repeat behind.

35

One-Headed Dragon

Two-Headed Dragon

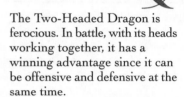

The Two-Headed Dragon is ferocious. In battle, with its heads working together, it has a winning advantage since it can be offensive and defensive at the same time.

Carry two shields and a sword. Challenge the monster to a riddle: ask it which head is better. As both are fiercely competitive, it will battle itself till one head wins. While watching the battle, place your sword on the ground. The winning head, seeing no danger, will protect you from its other head.

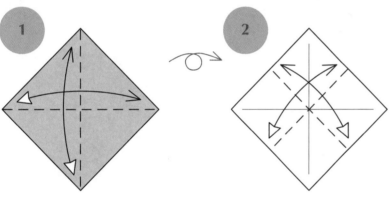

Fold and unfold.

Fold and unfold.

Fold to the center and unfold. Rotate.

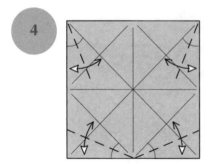

Fold and unfold.

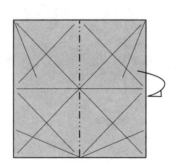

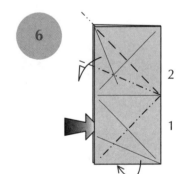

1. Reverse-fold.
2. Crimp-fold.
Rotate.

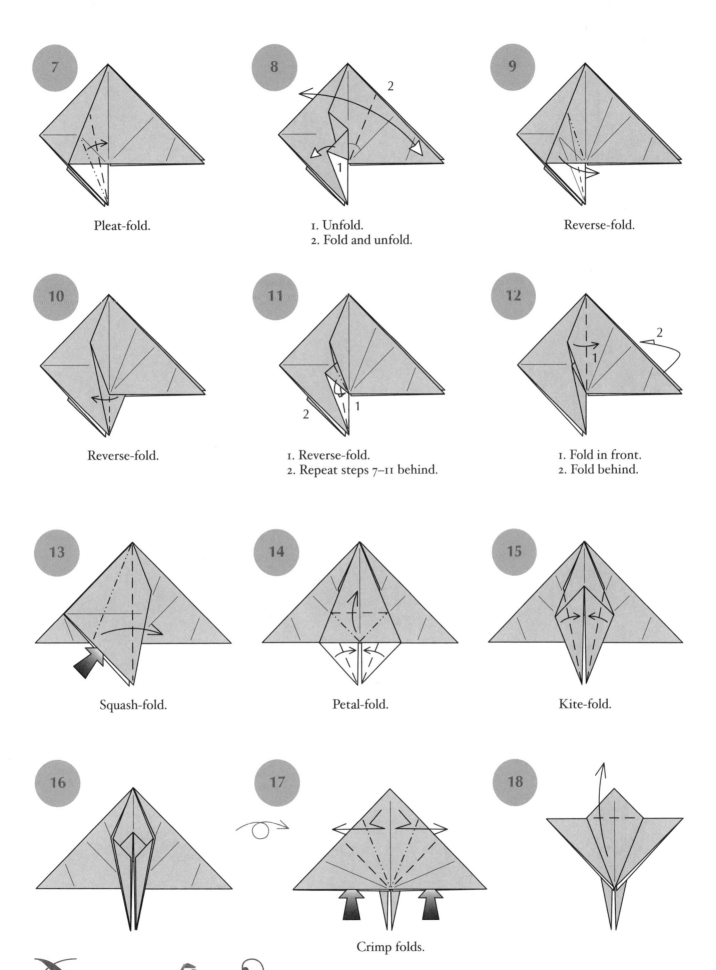

7 Pleat-fold.

8
1. Unfold.
2. Fold and unfold.

9 Reverse-fold.

10 Reverse-fold.

11
1. Reverse-fold.
2. Repeat steps 7–11 behind.

12
1. Fold in front.
2. Fold behind.

13 Squash-fold.

14 Petal-fold.

15 Kite-fold.

16

17 Crimp folds.

18

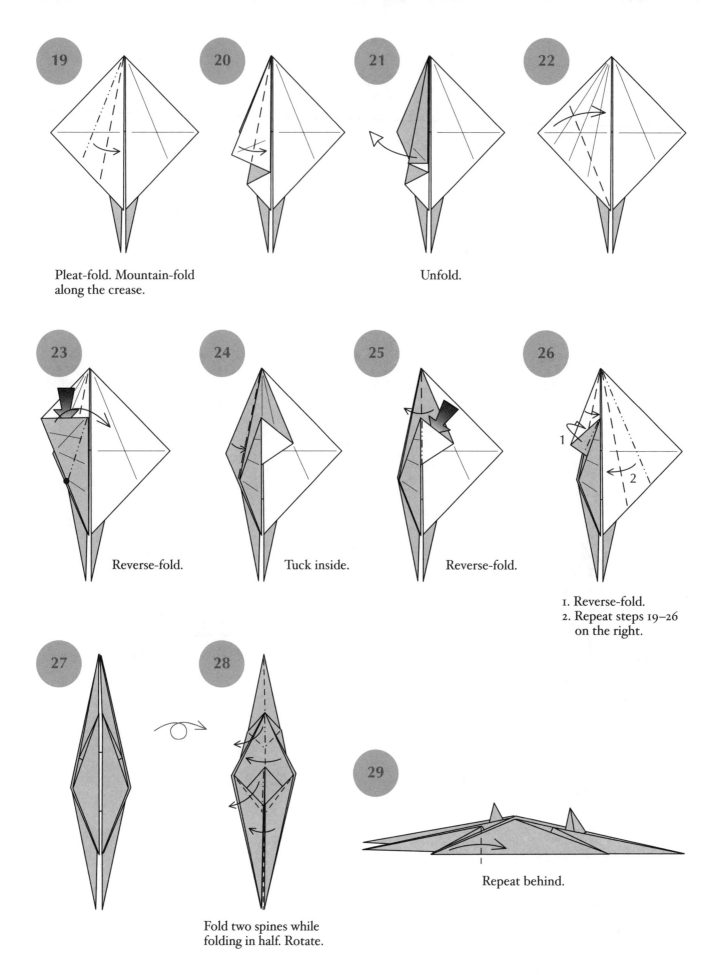

19 Pleat-fold. Mountain-fold along the crease.

21 Unfold.

23 Reverse-fold.

24 Tuck inside.

25 Reverse-fold.

26
1. Reverse-fold.
2. Repeat steps 19–26 on the right.

28 Fold two spines while folding in half. Rotate.

29 Repeat behind.

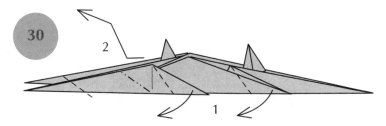

30

1. Fold the legs.
2. Reverse folds.
Repeat behind.

31

1. Spread the head.
2. Reverse folds.
Repeat behind.

32

1. Reverse-fold, repeat behind.
2. Reverse folds, repeat behind.
3. Pleat-fold.
4. Pleat-fold.

33

Two-Headed Dragon

Three-Headed Dragon

The Three-Headed Dragon is very dangerous. Not many who encounter it live to tell their tale.

If you bring a sword or ax, the three heads will surround you, snatch your weapons, and you, too. To capture this one, use your staff to call the One-Headed Dragon, and bring the captured Two-Headed Dragon. They will link to resemble a three-headed dragon. The Three-Headed Dragon will think there is another of its kind. Then you can use your staff to capture it.

1

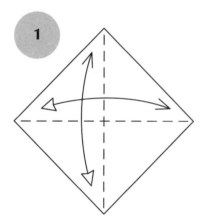

Fold and unfold.

2

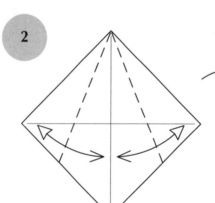

Kite-fold and unfold.

3

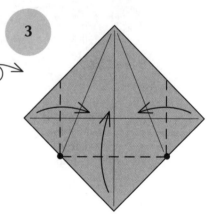

4

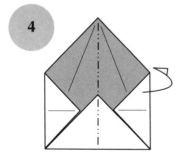

Fold in half.

5

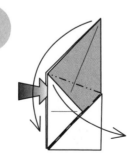

Squash-fold. Rotate.

6

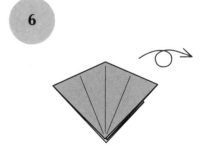

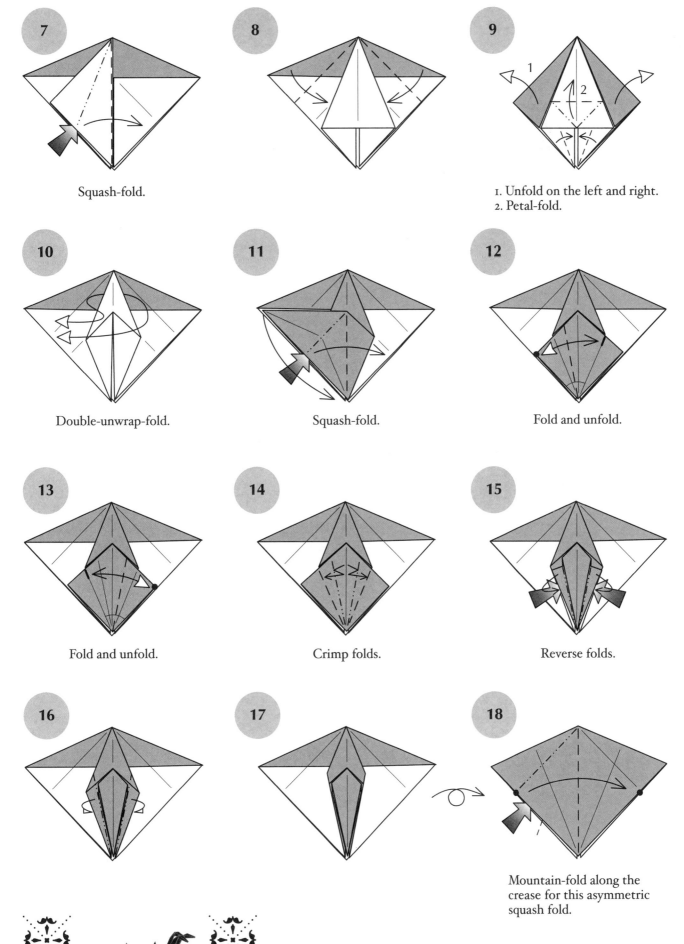

7 Squash-fold.

8

9 1. Unfold on the left and right.
2. Petal-fold.

10 Double-unwrap-fold.

11 Squash-fold.

12 Fold and unfold.

13 Fold and unfold.

14 Crimp folds.

15 Reverse folds.

16

17

18 Mountain-fold along the crease for this asymmetric squash fold.

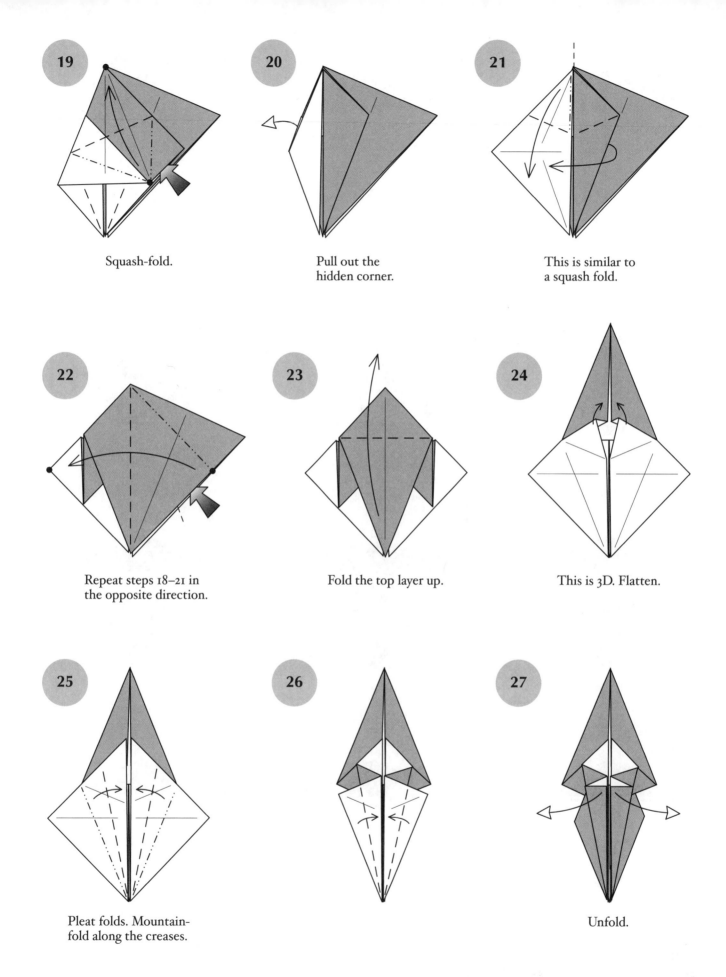

19 Squash-fold.

20 Pull out the hidden corner.

21 This is similar to a squash fold.

22 Repeat steps 18–21 in the opposite direction.

23 Fold the top layer up.

24 This is 3D. Flatten.

25 Pleat folds. Mountain-fold along the creases.

26

27 Unfold.

Dragons and Other Fantastic Creatures in Origami

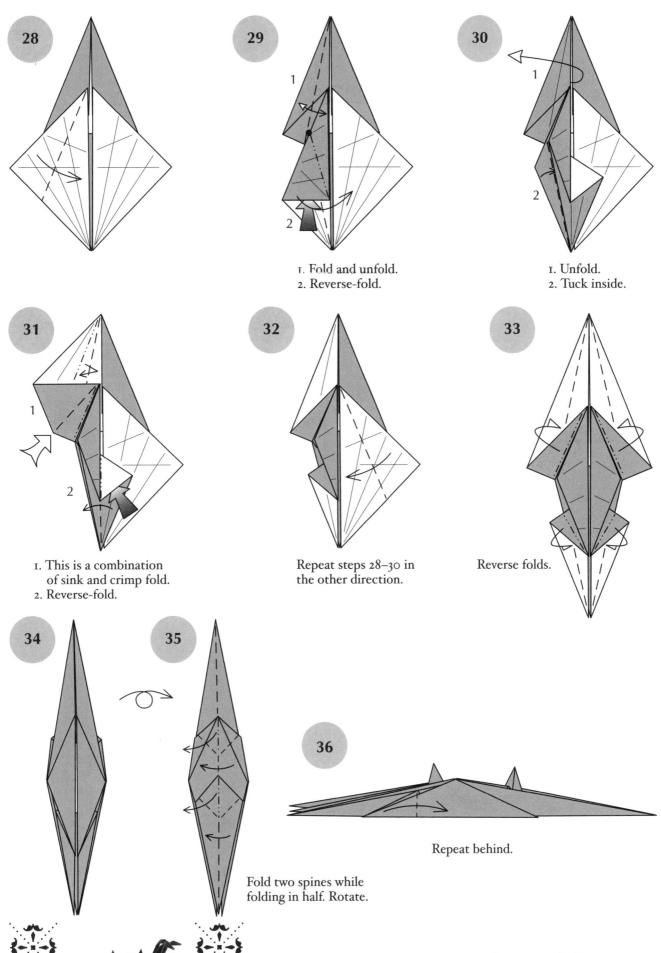

28

29

1. Fold and unfold.
2. Reverse-fold.

30

1. Unfold.
2. Tuck inside.

31

1. This is a combination
   of sink and crimp fold.
2. Reverse-fold.

32

Repeat steps 28–30 in
the other direction.

33

Reverse folds.

34

35

Fold two spines while
folding in half. Rotate.

36

Repeat behind.

37

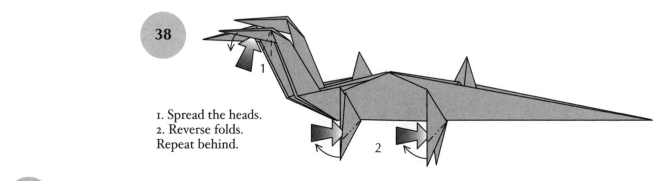

1. Fold the legs, repeat behind.
2. Three pairs of reverse folds. The necks can be at different angles.

38

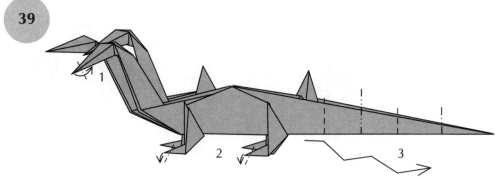

1. Spread the heads.
2. Reverse folds. Repeat behind.

39

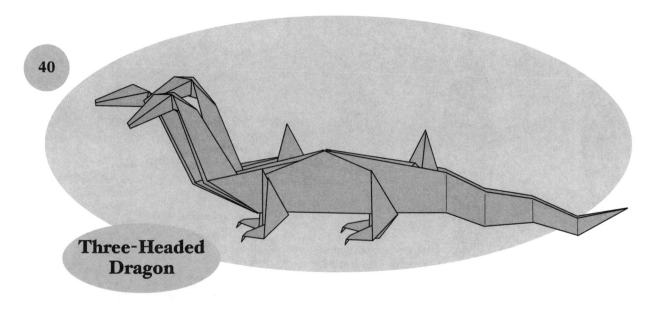

1. Reverse-fold, repeat two times.
2. Reverse folds, repeat behind.
3. Pleat-fold.

40

Three-Headed Dragon

Medieval Dragon

The Medieval Dragon was a peaceful creature. Practically forgotten, we are lucky to revive it here in the Forest. DNA testing shows this dragon to be the precursor to the Traditional Crane (see steps 28-29). Once the crane became popular, the Medieval Dragon was forgotten.

Walk slowly to this creature with your sword, ax, and staff. Offer your sword and the Medieval Dragon will slice a square off the Enchanted Paper Tree. You must take that square, fold the traditional crane, and present it to the dragon. The dragon will then give you the power of flight. However, if this turns out not to be a Medieval Dragon, and you have offered your sword, you will quickly need to use your ax.

1

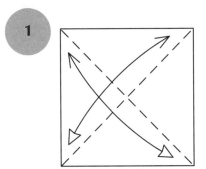

Fold and unfold.

2

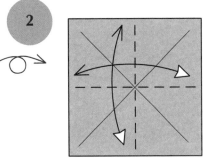

Fold and unfold.

3

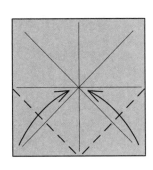

4

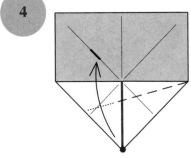

Bring the dot to the line.
Crease on the right.

5

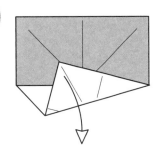

Unfold.

6

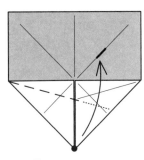

Repeat steps
4–5 on the left.

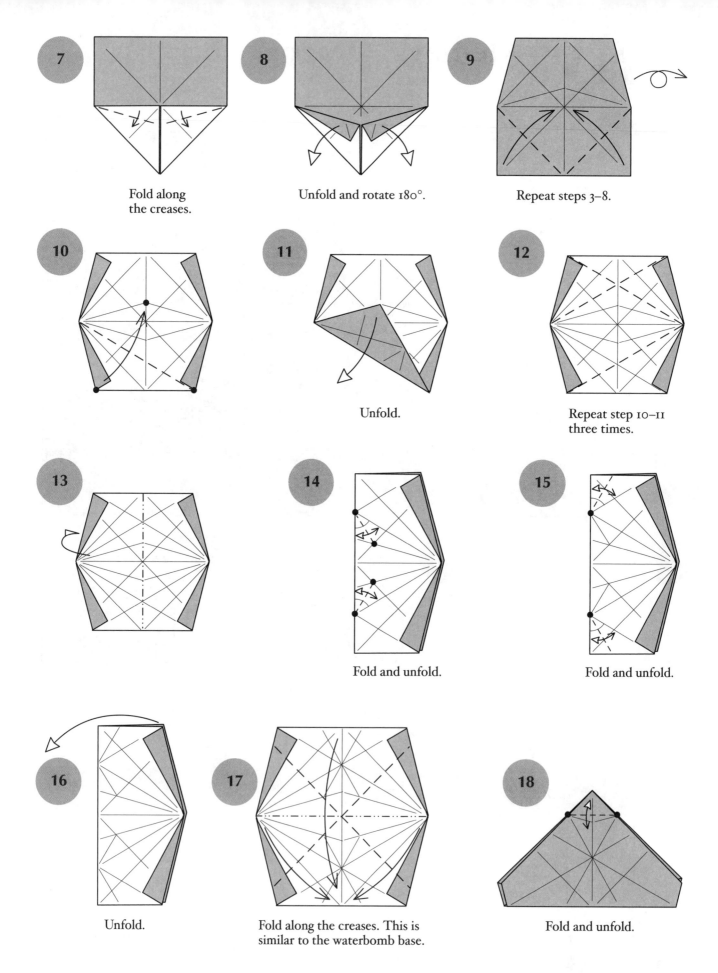

7 Fold along the creases.

8 Unfold and rotate 180°.

9 Repeat steps 3–8.

10

11 Unfold.

12 Repeat step 10–11 three times.

13

14 Fold and unfold.

15 Fold and unfold.

16 Unfold.

17 Fold along the creases. This is similar to the waterbomb base.

18 Fold and unfold.

19

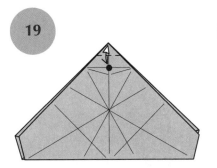

Fold and unfold.

20

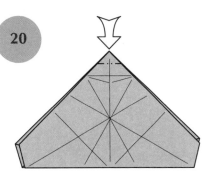

Sink.

21

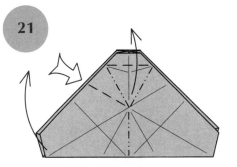

This is similar to a petal fold.

22

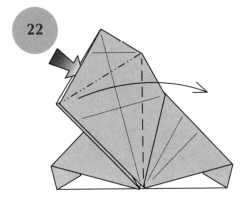

Squash-fold.

23

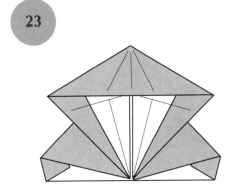

Repeat steps 21–22 behind.

24

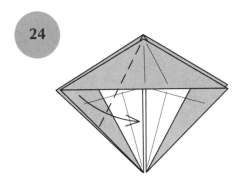

Reverse-fold.

25

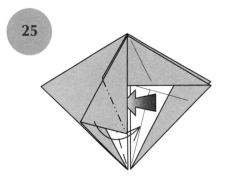

Reverse-fold.

26

Reverse-fold.

27

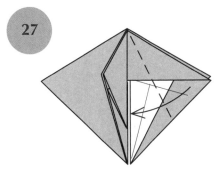

Repeat steps 24–26 three times, on the right and behind.

Medieval Dragon 39

28

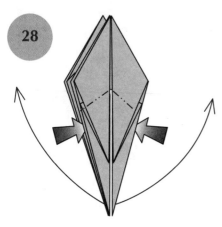

Reverse folds.

29

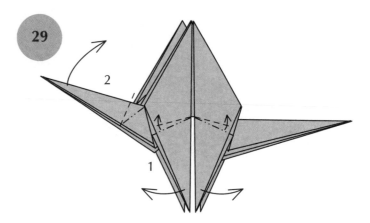

1. Bend the legs, repeat behind.
2. Crimp-fold.
Rotate.

30

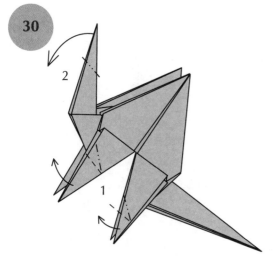

1. Crimp folds, repeat behind.
2. Reverse-fold.

31

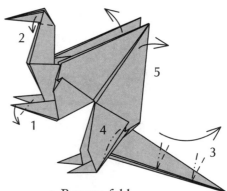

1. Reverse-fold.
2. Fold the top layer.
3. Crimp folds.
4. Shape the hind legs.
5. Spread the wings.
Repeat behind.

32

Medieval Dragon

Dragon with Claws

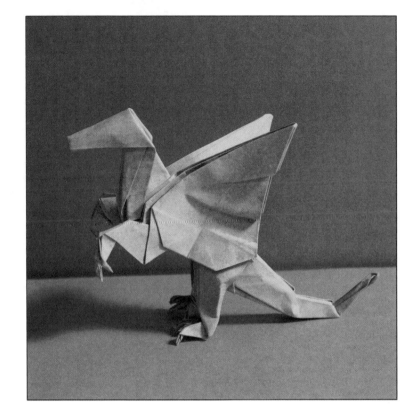

The Dragon with Claws is not very friendly. This dragon can run, jump, and fly very quickly, which is necessary for its voracious appetite.

This beast is lethargic in the morning, so use your sword to de-claw it then. Be careful to do it before you are its breakfast. Once declawed, the dragon will pose no threat.

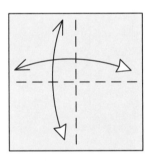

1   Fold and unfold.

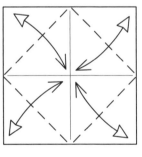

2   Fold to the center and unfold.

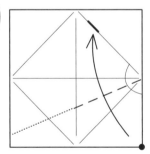

3   Crease on the right.

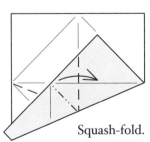

4   Squash-fold.

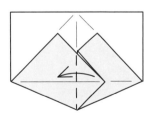

5

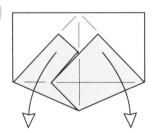

6   Unfold and rotate 180°.

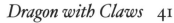

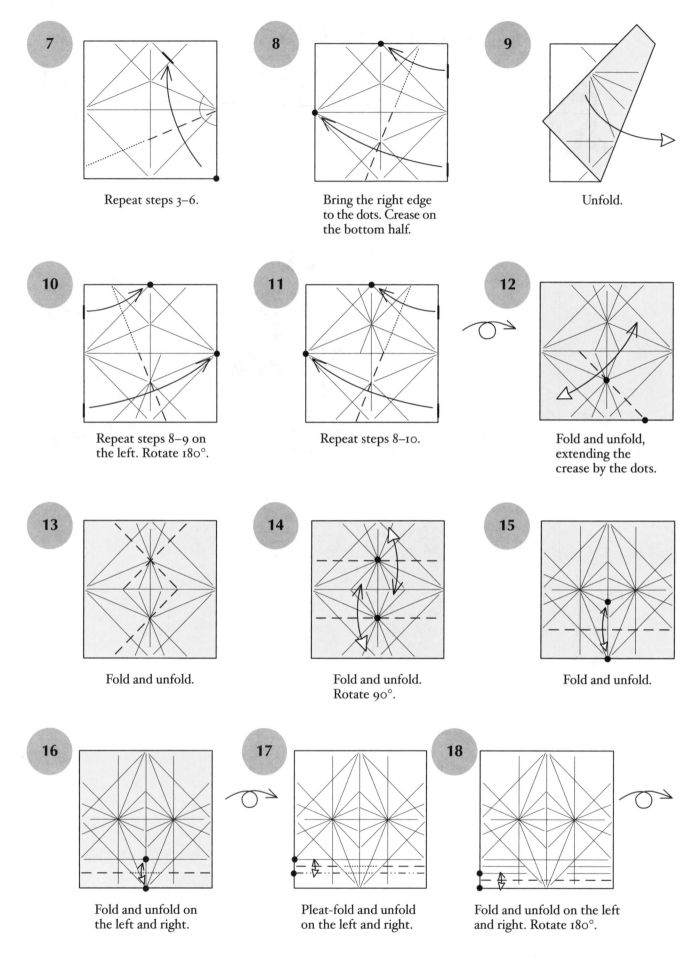

7

Repeat steps 3–6.

8

Bring the right edge to the dots. Crease on the bottom half.

9

Unfold.

10

Repeat steps 8–9 on the left. Rotate 180°.

11

Repeat steps 8–10.

12

Fold and unfold, extending the crease by the dots.

13

Fold and unfold.

14

Fold and unfold. Rotate 90°.

15

Fold and unfold.

16

Fold and unfold on the left and right.

17

Pleat-fold and unfold on the left and right.

18

Fold and unfold on the left and right. Rotate 180°.

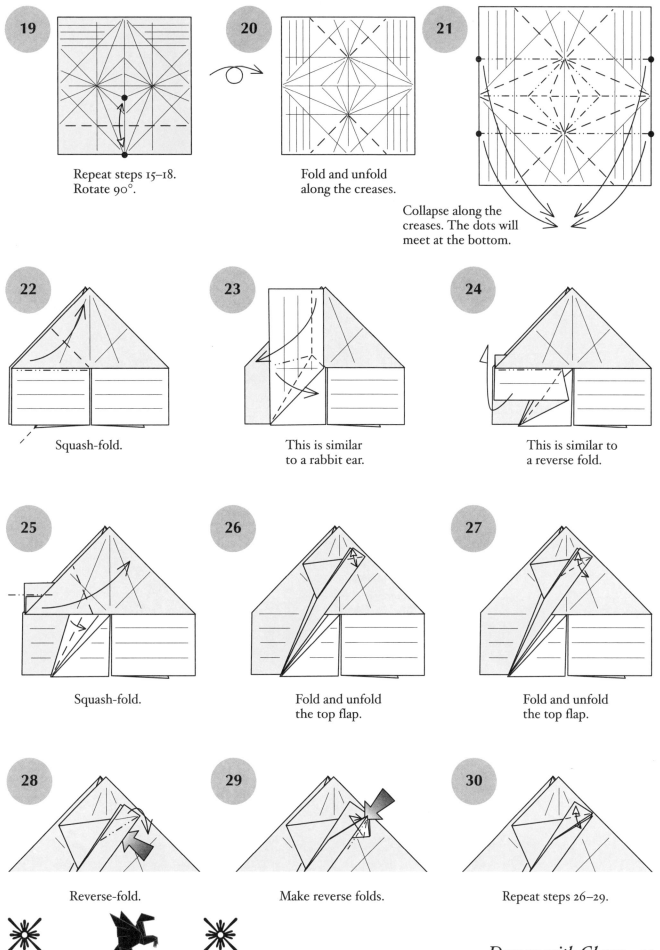

19 Repeat steps 15–18. Rotate 90°.

20 Fold and unfold along the creases.

21 Collapse along the creases. The dots will meet at the bottom.

22 Squash-fold.

23 This is similar to a rabbit ear.

24 This is similar to a reverse fold.

25 Squash-fold.

26 Fold and unfold the top flap.

27 Fold and unfold the top flap.

28 Reverse-fold.

29 Make reverse folds.

30 Repeat steps 26–29.

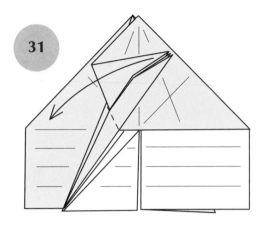

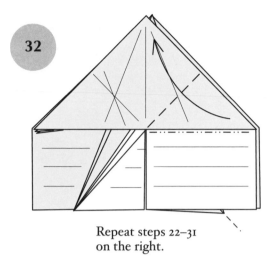

Repeat steps 22–31
on the right.

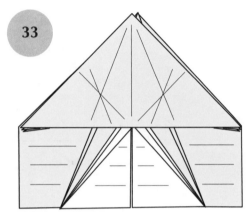

Repeat steps
22–32 behind.

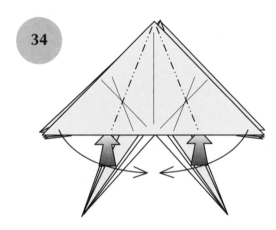

Reverse folds, repeat behind.

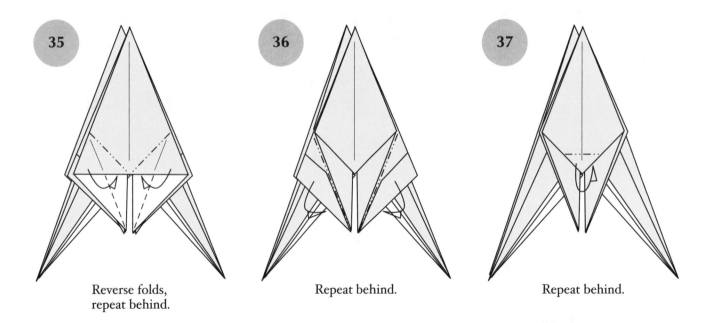

Reverse folds,
repeat behind.

Repeat behind.

Repeat behind.

44 *Dragons and Other Fantastic Creatures in Origami*

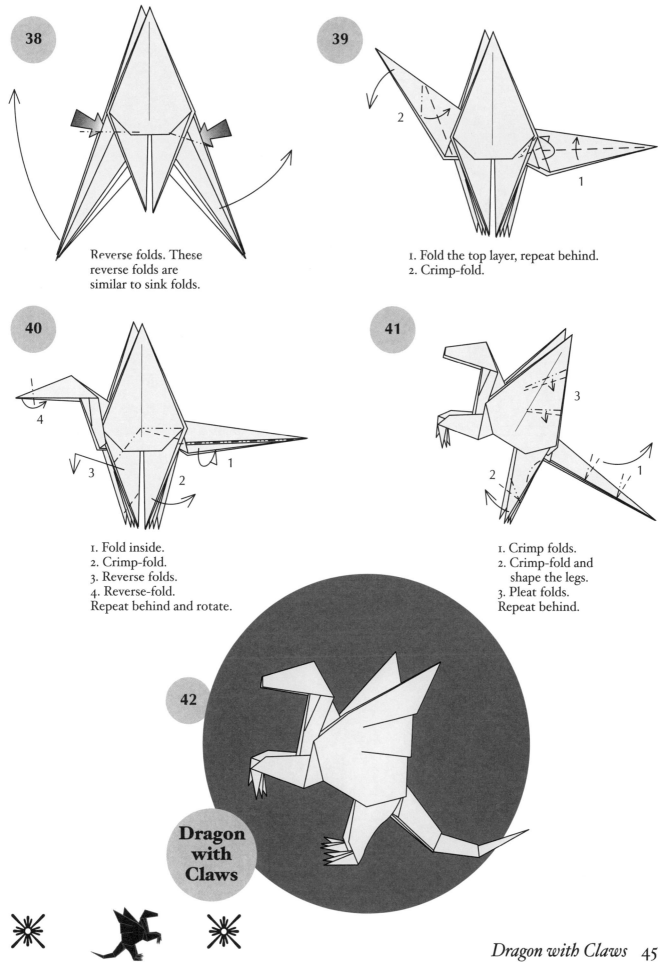

38

Reverse folds. These reverse folds are similar to sink folds.

39

1. Fold the top layer, repeat behind.
2. Crimp-fold.

40

1. Fold inside.
2. Crimp-fold.
3. Reverse folds.
4. Reverse-fold.
Repeat behind and rotate.

41

1. Crimp folds.
2. Crimp-fold and shape the legs.
3. Pleat folds.
Repeat behind.

42

Dragon with Claws

Standing Dragon

This fire-breathing dragon finds humans especially tasty. This delicacy, soft on the outside, crunchy on the inside, and with a spicy liver, make us a favorite treat.

Hide behind your shield and bring an ax. Clever as this dragon is, it has a poor inner ear. Walk around this creature a few times to make it dizzy. It will fall asleep and you can then capture it. It will wake up in about ten days, so have your ax ready.

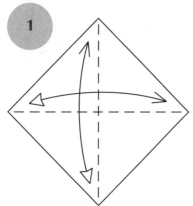

1

Fold and unfold.

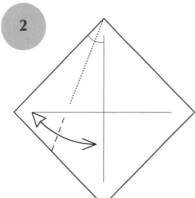

2

Fold and unfold on the left.

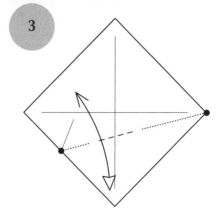

3

Fold and unfold on the diagonal.

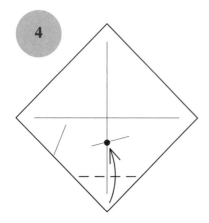

4

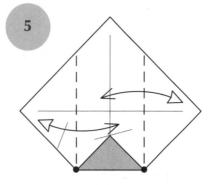

5

Fold and unfold.

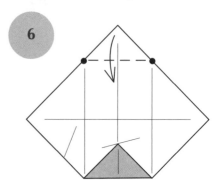

6

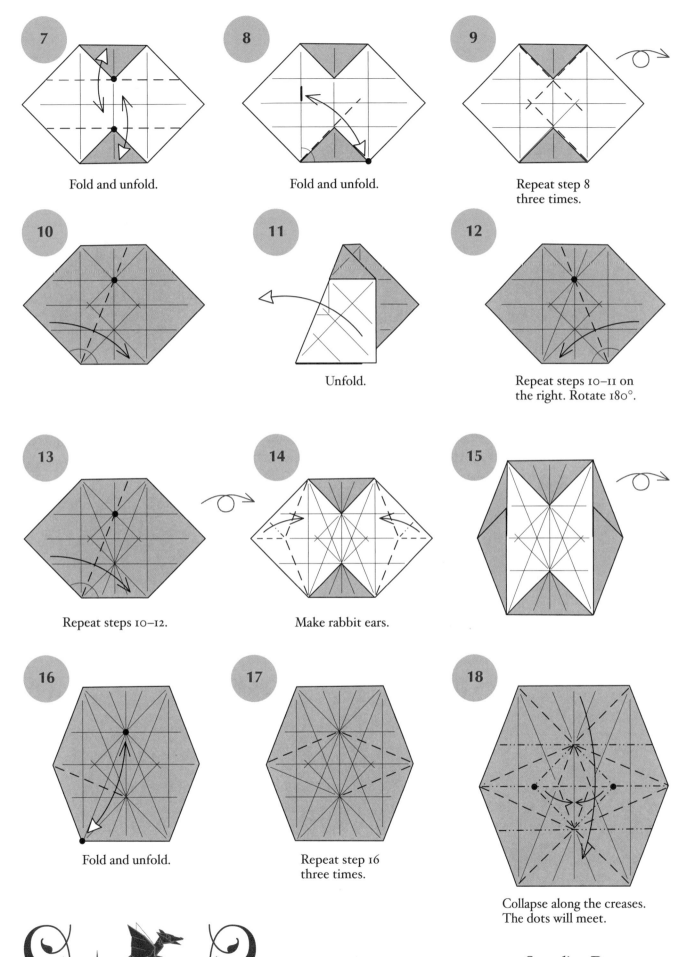

7 Fold and unfold.

8 Fold and unfold.

9 Repeat step 8 three times.

10

11 Unfold.

12 Repeat steps 10–11 on the right. Rotate 180°.

13 Repeat steps 10–12.

14 Make rabbit ears.

15

16 Fold and unfold.

17 Repeat step 16 three times.

18 Collapse along the creases. The dots will meet.

Standing Dragon 47

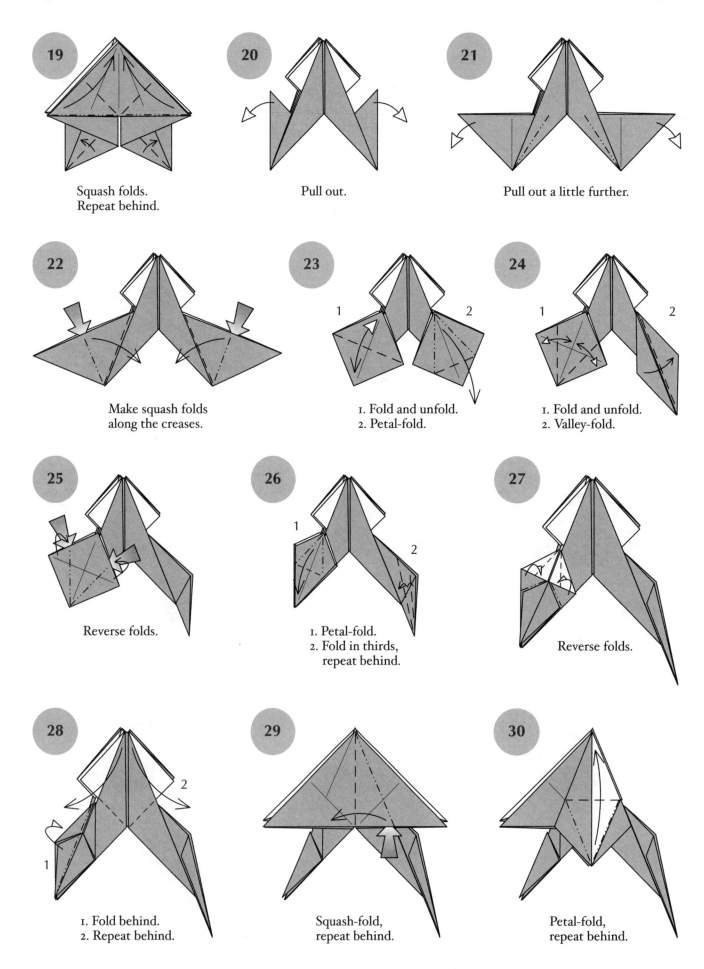

19

Squash folds.
Repeat behind.

20

Pull out.

21

Pull out a little further.

22

Make squash folds
along the creases.

23

1. Fold and unfold.
2. Petal-fold.

24

1. Fold and unfold.
2. Valley-fold.

25

Reverse folds.

26

1. Petal-fold.
2. Fold in thirds,
   repeat behind.

27

Reverse folds.

28

1. Fold behind.
2. Repeat behind.

29

Squash-fold,
repeat behind.

30

Petal-fold,
repeat behind.

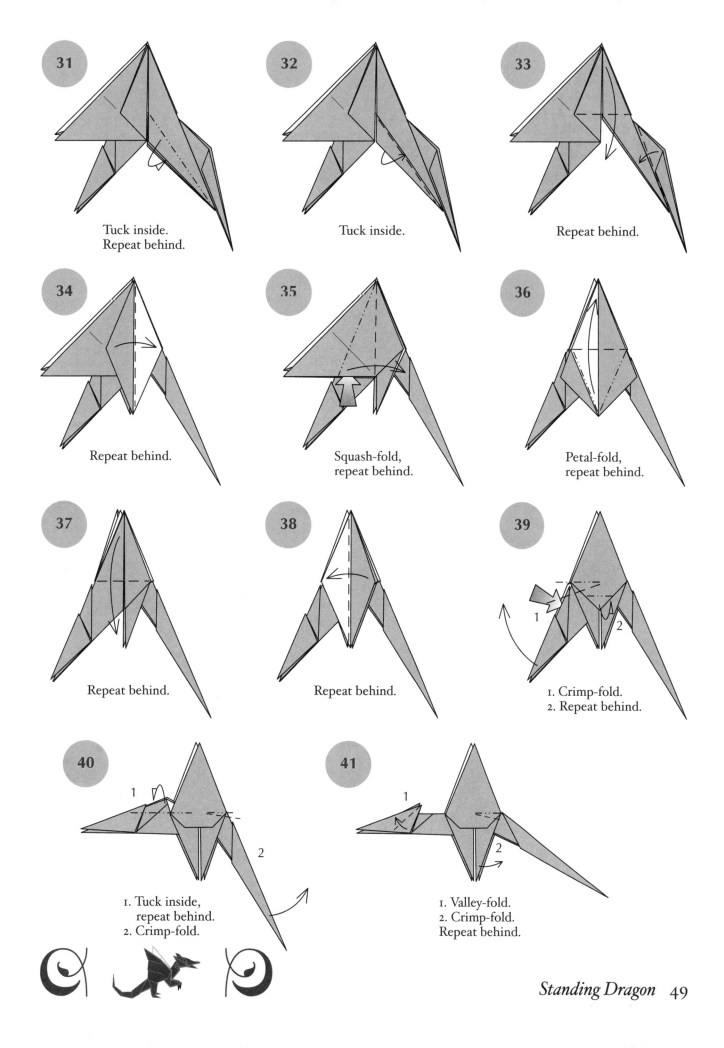

31 Tuck inside. Repeat behind.

32 Tuck inside.

33 Repeat behind.

34 Repeat behind.

35 Squash-fold, repeat behind.

36 Petal-fold, repeat behind.

37 Repeat behind.

38 Repeat behind.

39 1. Crimp-fold. 2. Repeat behind.

40 1. Tuck inside, repeat behind. 2. Crimp-fold.

41 1. Valley-fold. 2. Crimp-fold. Repeat behind.

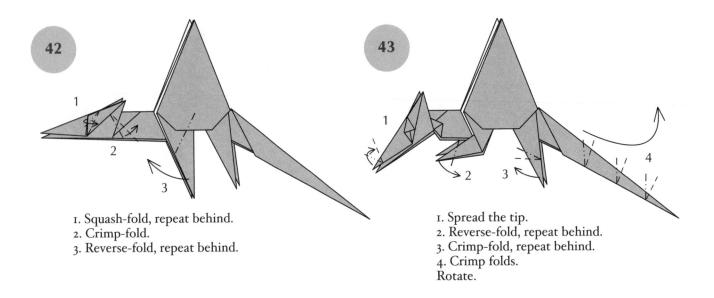

42

1. Squash-fold, repeat behind.
2. Crimp-fold.
3. Reverse-fold, repeat behind.

43

1. Spread the tip.
2. Reverse-fold, repeat behind.
3. Crimp-fold, repeat behind.
4. Crimp folds.
Rotate.

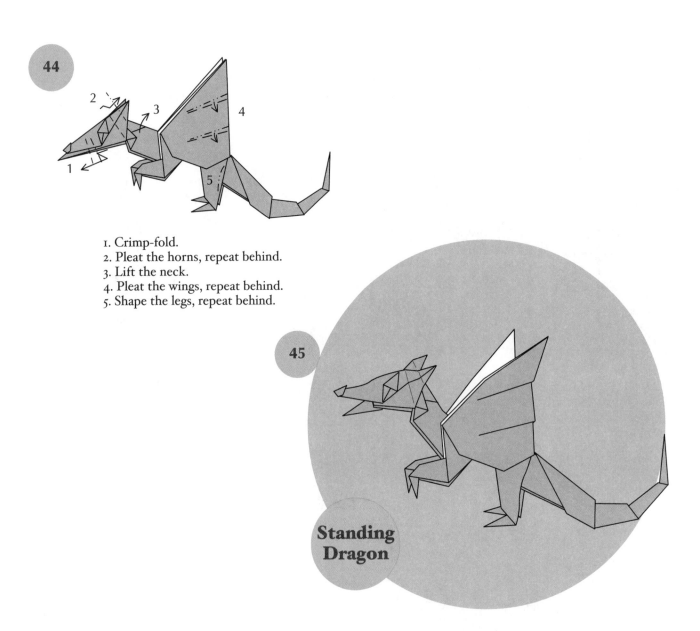

44

1. Crimp-fold.
2. Pleat the horns, repeat behind.
3. Lift the neck.
4. Pleat the wings, repeat behind.
5. Shape the legs, repeat behind.

45

Standing Dragon

Chinese Dragon

Though wingless, the Chinese Dragon is an agile flier. It will appear on many festive occasions.

To capture it, wait for an eclipse of the Sun. The dragon will eat the Sun and all will be covered in darkness. Use your staff then to capture it in the dark. Once captured, you will have the power of the Sun and Moon. If you have the power of flight, you can fly to the Moon. But you probably should not attempt to fly to the Sun during the day, perhaps at night it might be OK.

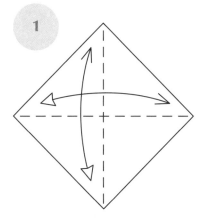

Fold and unfold.

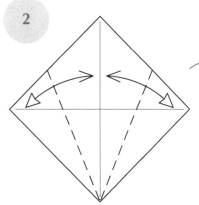

Kite-fold and unfold.

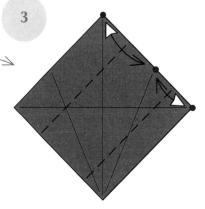

Fold and unfold.

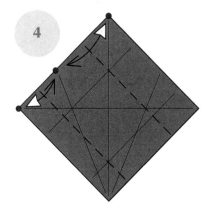

Fold and unfold.

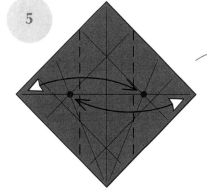

Fold and unfold.

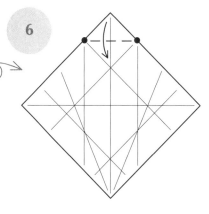

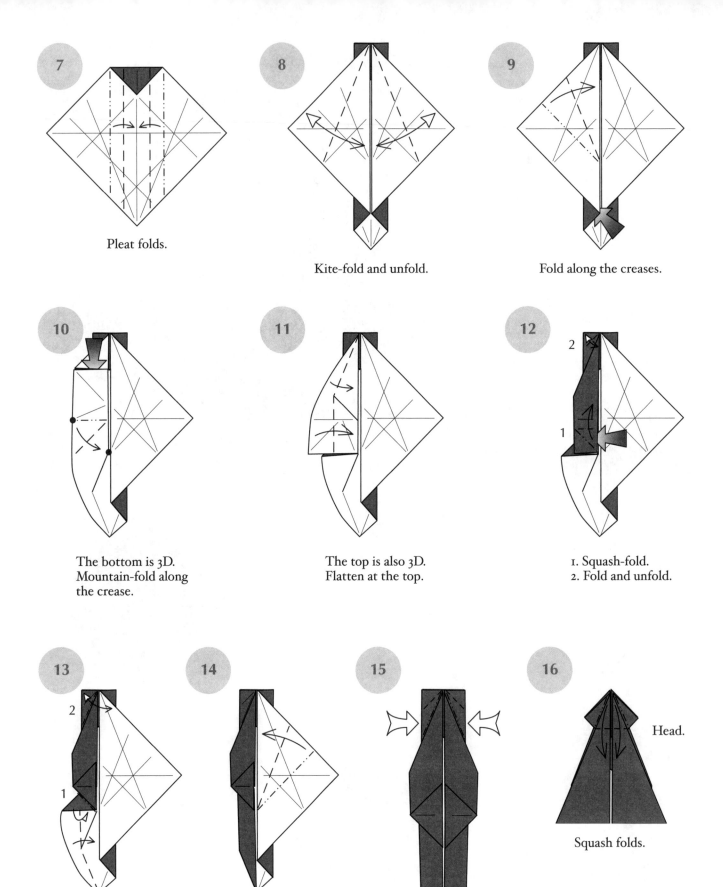

7 Pleat folds.

8 Kite-fold and unfold.

9 Fold along the creases.

10 The bottom is 3D. Mountain-fold along the crease.

11 The top is also 3D. Flatten at the top.

12 1. Squash-fold. 2. Fold and unfold.

13 1. Reverse-fold and flatten. 2. Fold and unfold.

14 Repeat steps 9–13 on the right.

15 Crimp folds.

16 Head. Squash folds.

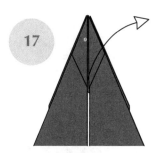

17

Pull out the
hidden corner.

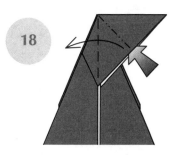

18

Squash-fold.

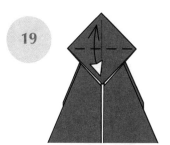

19

Fold and unfold.

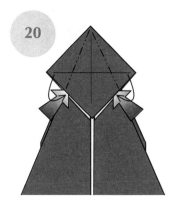

20

Reverse folds.

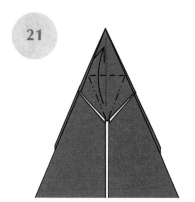

21

Petal-fold.

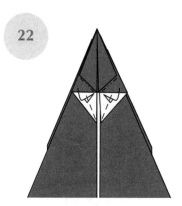

22

Reverse folds.

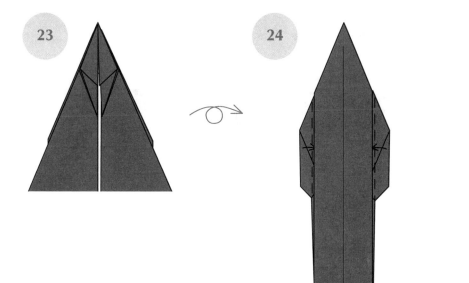

23

24

Tuck inside.

25

Do not crease
at the top.

Chinese Dragon 53

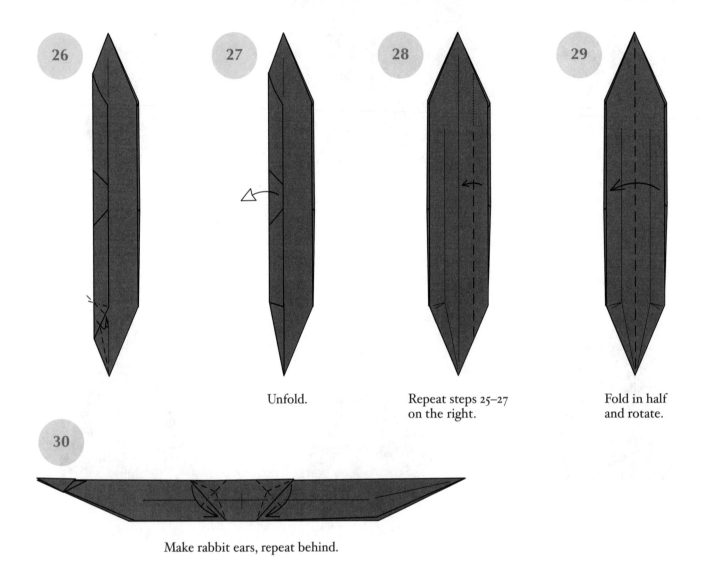

26

27

Unfold.

28

Repeat steps 25–27
on the right.

29

Fold in half
and rotate.

30

Make rabbit ears, repeat behind.

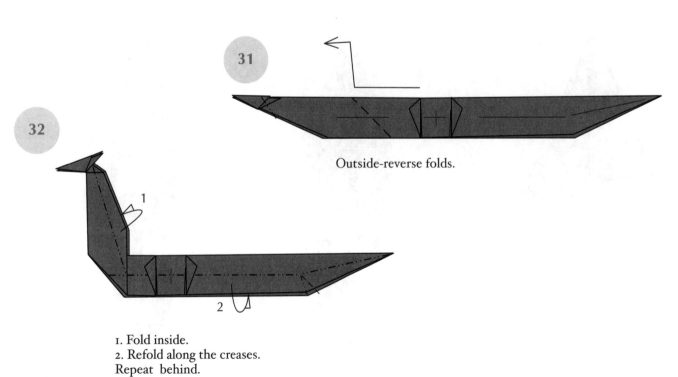

31

Outside-reverse folds.

32

1. Fold inside.
2. Refold along the creases.
Repeat behind.

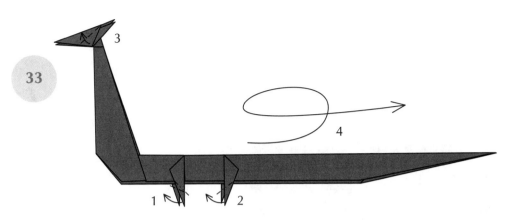

33

1. Crimp-fold.
2. Reverse-fold.
3. Valley-fold.
4. Curl the tail a few times
   around, then let go.
Repeat behind at 1, 2, and 3.

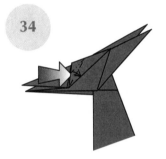

34

Spread-squash-fold,
repeat behind.

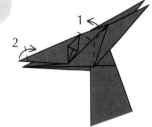

35

1. Rabbit-ear, repeat behind.
2. Outside-reverse-fold
   and spread.

36

1. Crimp-fold.
2. Repeat behind.

37

**Chinese
Dragon**

Western Dragon

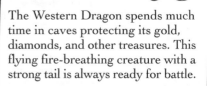

The Western Dragon spends much time in caves protecting its gold, diamonds, and other treasures. This flying fire-breathing creature with a strong tail is always ready for battle.

Hide behind your shield as you wield your sword. While protected by your shield, the dragon will breath fire towards you. When the fire hits your sword, it will become a singing sword. Move the sword to start it singing and soon the dragon will sing along. In its merriment, the dragon will give you a small jewel and will sing for you anytime you wish.

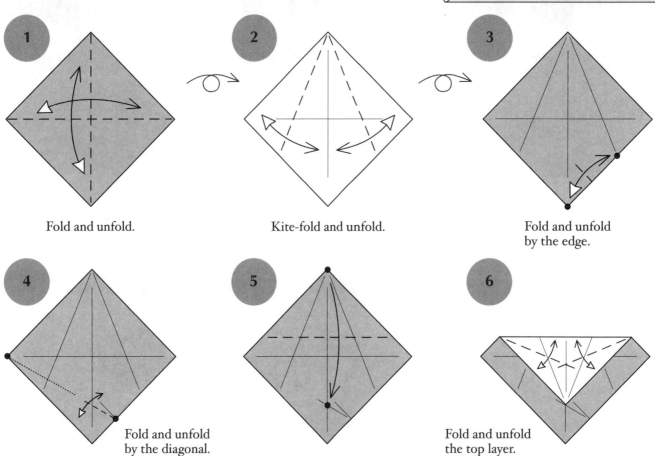

1 Fold and unfold.

2 Kite-fold and unfold.

3 Fold and unfold by the edge.

4 Fold and unfold by the diagonal.

5

6 Fold and unfold the top layer.

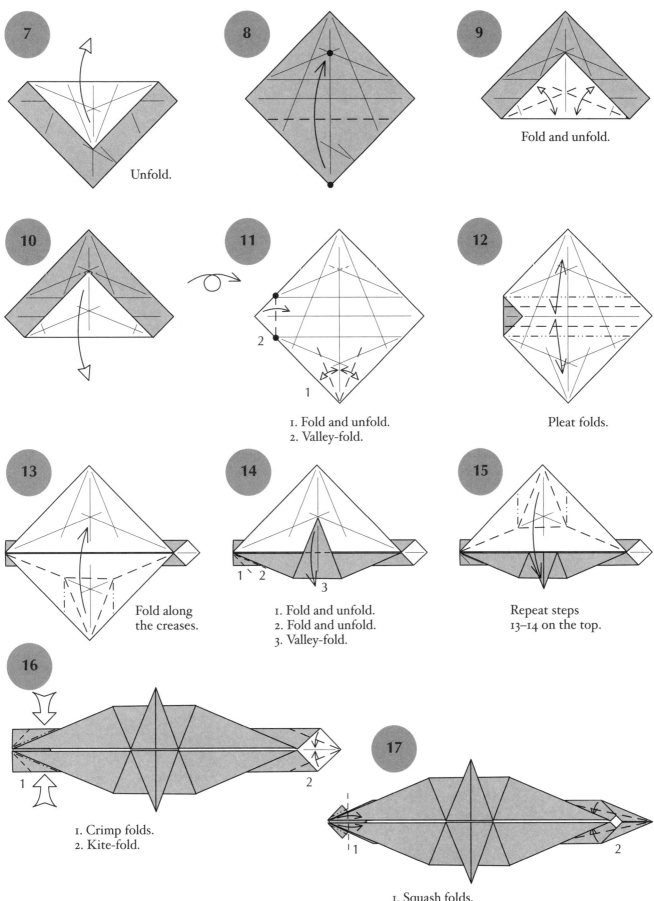

7 Unfold.

8

9 Fold and unfold.

10

11
1. Fold and unfold.
2. Valley-fold.

12 Pleat folds.

13 Fold along the creases.

14
1. Fold and unfold.
2. Fold and unfold.
3. Valley-fold.

15 Repeat steps 13–14 on the top.

16
1. Crimp folds.
2. Kite-fold.

17
1. Squash folds.
2. Fold to the center and tuck inside.

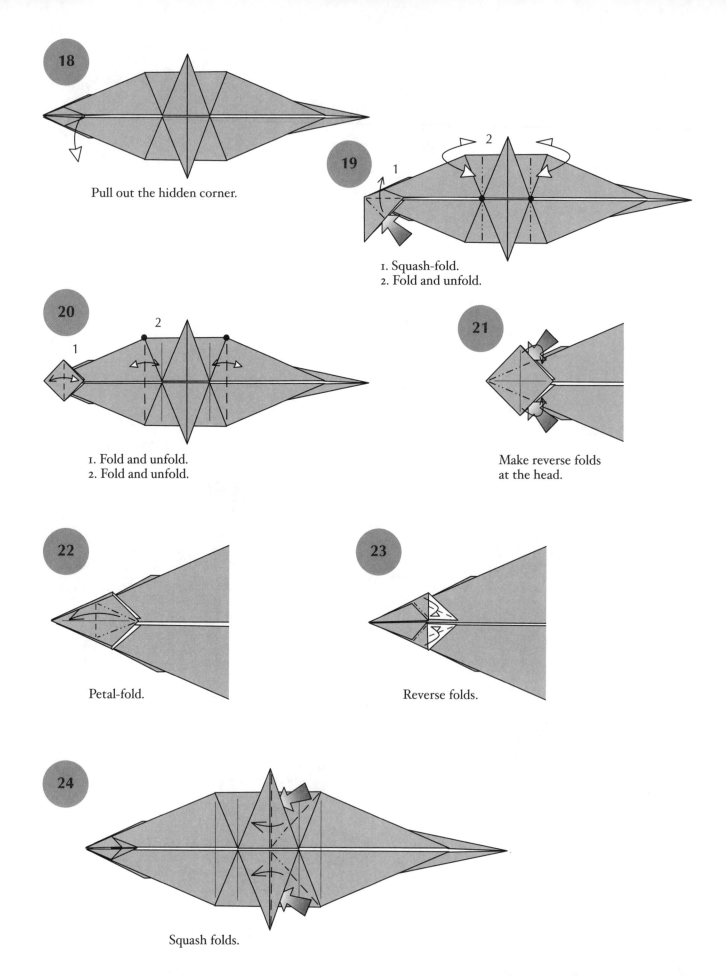

18

Pull out the hidden corner.

19

1. Squash-fold.
2. Fold and unfold.

20

1. Fold and unfold.
2. Fold and unfold.

21

Make reverse folds
at the head.

22

Petal-fold.

23

Reverse folds.

24

Squash folds.

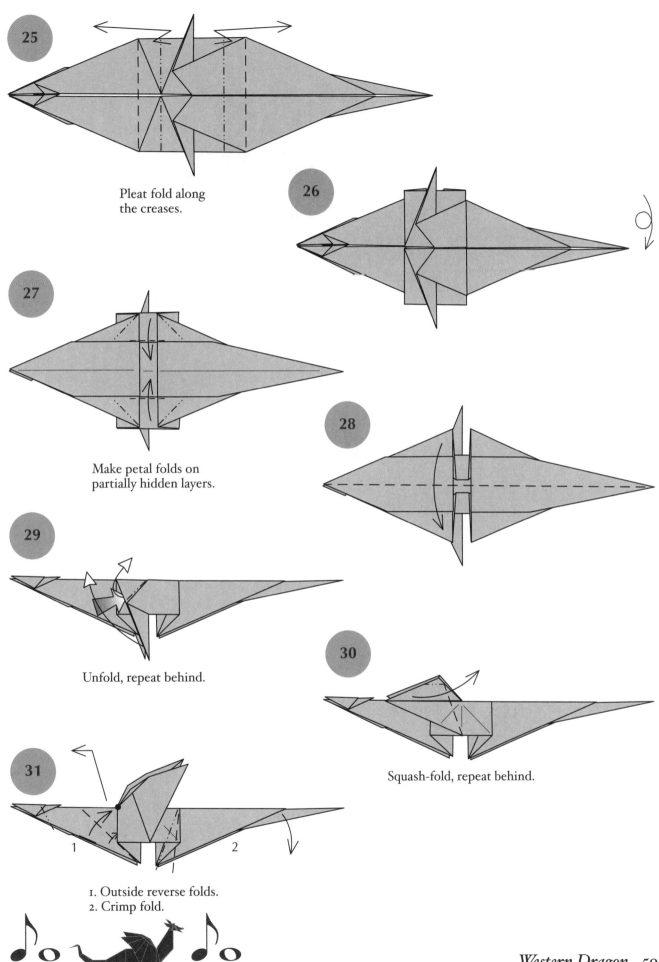

25

Pleat fold along the creases.

26

27

Make petal folds on partially hidden layers.

28

29

Unfold, repeat behind.

30

Squash-fold, repeat behind.

31

1. Outside reverse folds.
2. Crimp fold.

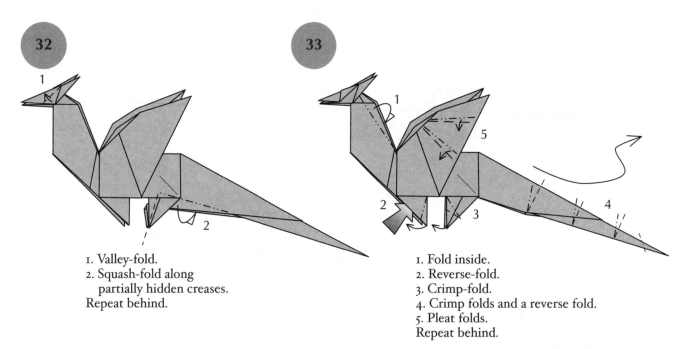

32

1.
2.

1. Valley-fold.
2. Squash-fold along
   partially hidden creases.
Repeat behind.

33

1.
2.
3.
4.
5.

1. Fold inside.
2. Reverse-fold.
3. Crimp-fold.
4. Crimp folds and a reverse fold.
5. Pleat folds.
Repeat behind.

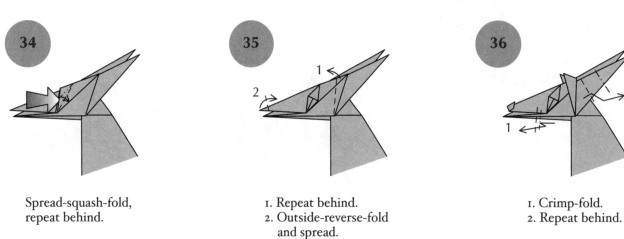

34

Spread-squash-fold,
repeat behind.

35

1.
2.

1. Repeat behind.
2. Outside-reverse-fold
   and spread.

36

1.
2.

1. Crimp-fold.
2. Repeat behind.

37

**Western
Dragon**

Western Dragon with Horns

The Western Dragon with Horns is much bigger and more fierce than other Western Dragons. Even your shield would be no match for its powers.

Still, it also likes to sing. Ask a singing dragon to accompany you while meeting this one. This dragon will then start singing, and will give you a ride between its horns. However, its singing voice will be a new experience for you and earplugs are highly suggested.

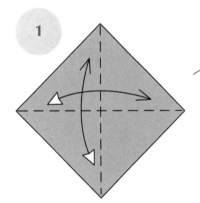

1 Fold and unfold.

2 Kite-fold and unfold.

3 Fold and unfold.

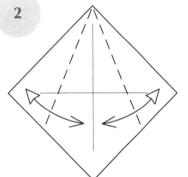

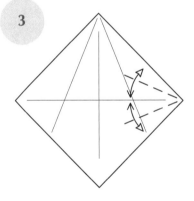

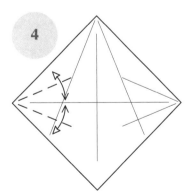

4 Fold and unfold.

5

6 Fold and unfold.

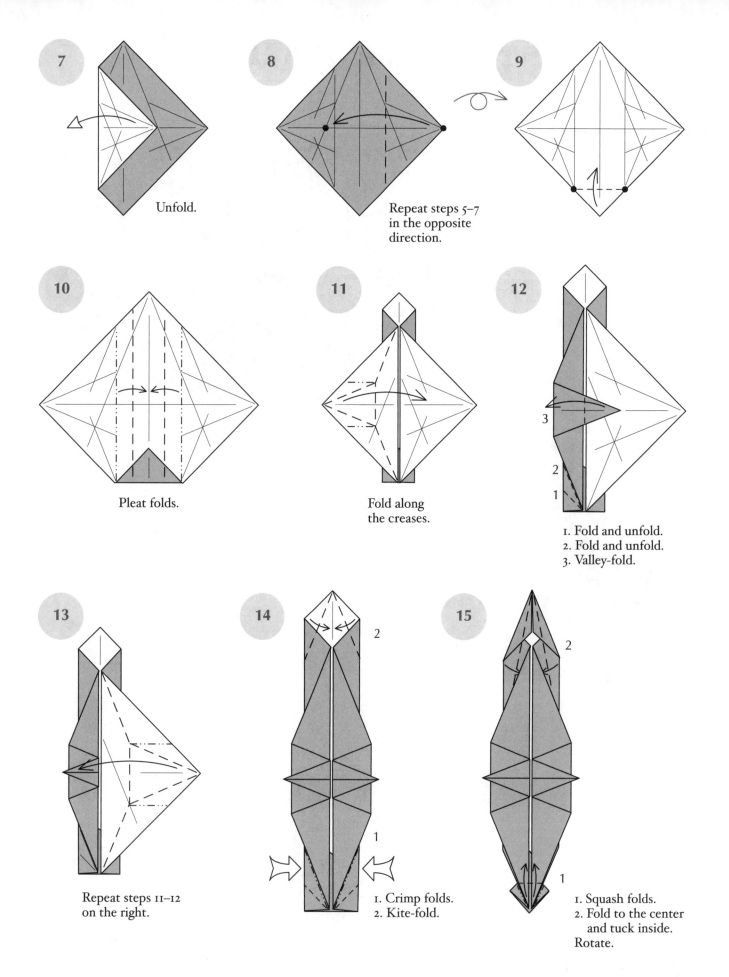

7 Unfold.

8 Repeat steps 5–7 in the opposite direction.

9

10 Pleat folds.

11 Fold along the creases.

12
1. Fold and unfold.
2. Fold and unfold.
3. Valley-fold.

13 Repeat steps 11–12 on the right.

14
1. Crimp folds.
2. Kite-fold.

15
1. Squash folds.
2. Fold to the center and tuck inside.
Rotate.

16

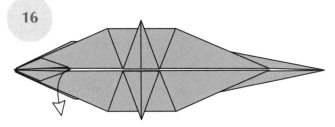

Pull out the hidden corner.

17

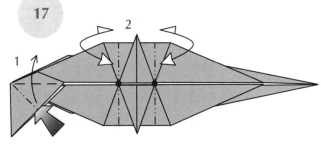

1. Squash-fold.
2. Fold and unfold.

18

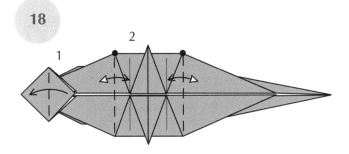

1. Fold the top layer.
2. Fold and unfold.

19

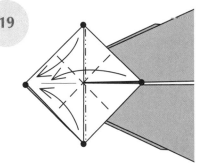

The dots will meet.

20

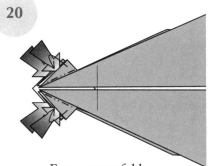

Four reverse folds.

21

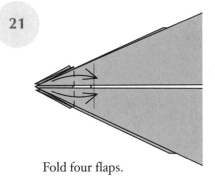

Fold four flaps.

22

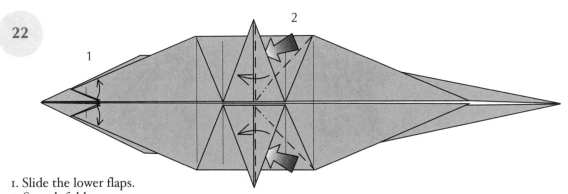

1. Slide the lower flaps.
2. Squash folds.

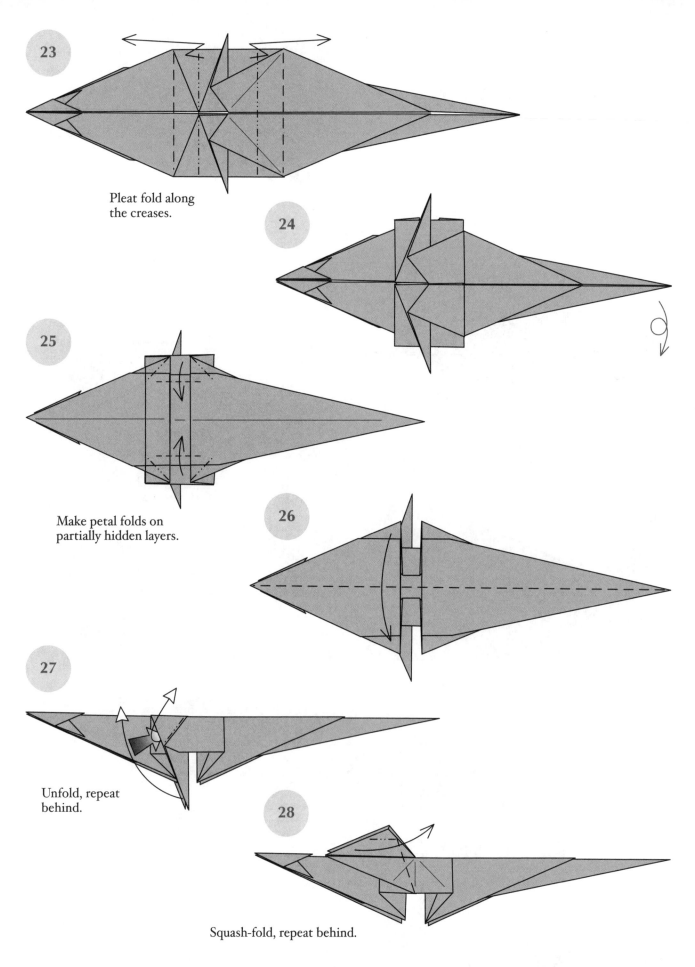

23

Pleat fold along
the creases.

24

25

Make petal folds on
partially hidden layers.

26

27

Unfold, repeat
behind.

28

Squash-fold, repeat behind.

Dragons and Other Fantastic Creatures in Origami

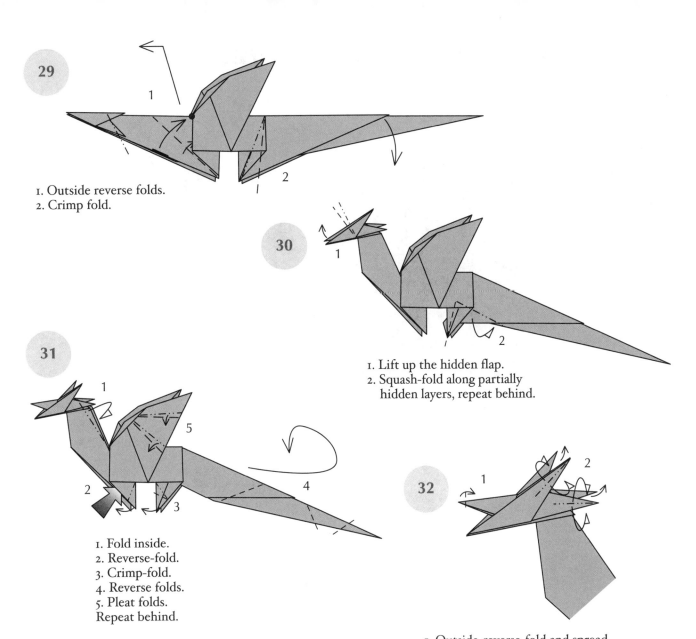

29

1. Outside reverse folds.
2. Crimp fold.

30

1. Lift up the hidden flap.
2. Squash-fold along partially
   hidden layers, repeat behind.

31

1. Fold inside.
2. Reverse-fold.
3. Crimp-fold.
4. Reverse folds.
5. Pleat folds.
Repeat behind.

32

1. Outside-reverse-fold and spread.
2. Thin and curl the horns, repeat behind.

33

Western Dragon with Horns

Three-Headed Standing Dragon

Danger! Danger! The final dragon to be captured is the ferocious fire-breathing, flying three-headed dragon. Even a shield is no match for the three heads. Many courageous warriors have tried, but nobody has lived to tell the tale.

Still, it is recommended that you bring your shield, sword, ax and staff, perhaps even two or three of each. Multitasking skills are essential. Should you survive and possess all the other dragons, you will become Master of the Enchanted Dragons.

1

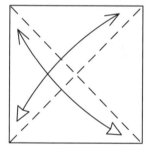

Fold and unfold.

2

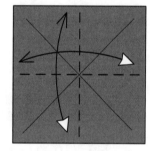

Fold and unfold.

3

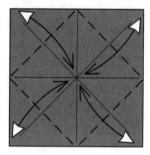

Fold and unfold.

4

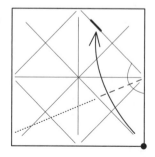

Bring the dot to the line.
Crease on the right.

5

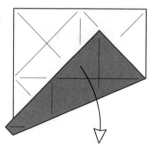

Unfold.

6

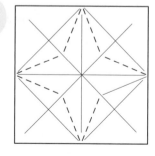

Repeat steps 4–5
seven times.

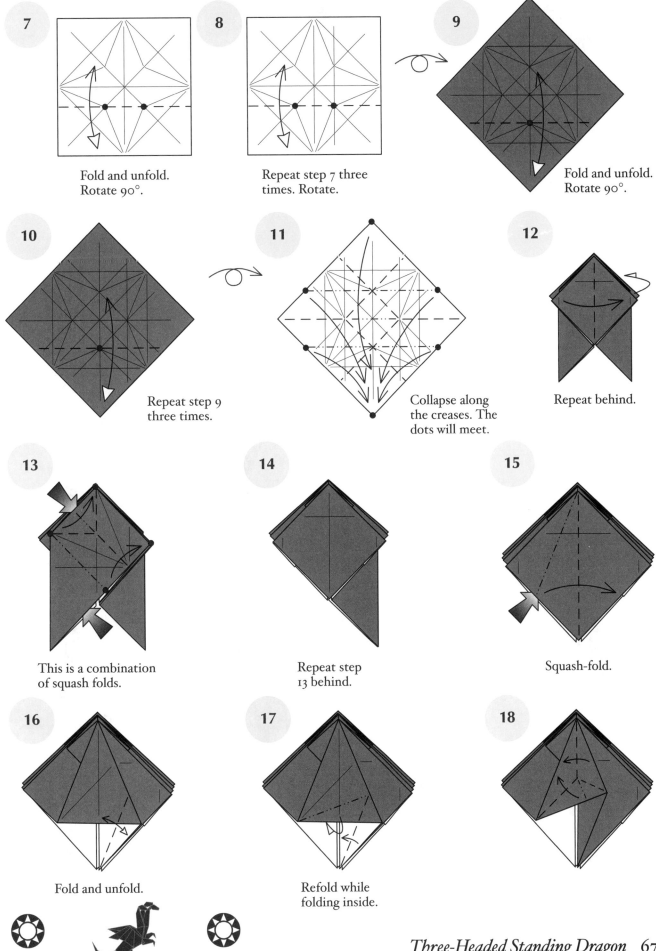

7 Fold and unfold. Rotate 90°.

8 Repeat step 7 three times. Rotate.

9 Fold and unfold. Rotate 90°.

10 Repeat step 9 three times.

11 Collapse along the creases. The dots will meet.

12 Repeat behind.

13 This is a combination of squash folds.

14 Repeat step 13 behind.

15 Squash-fold.

16 Fold and unfold.

17 Refold while folding inside.

18

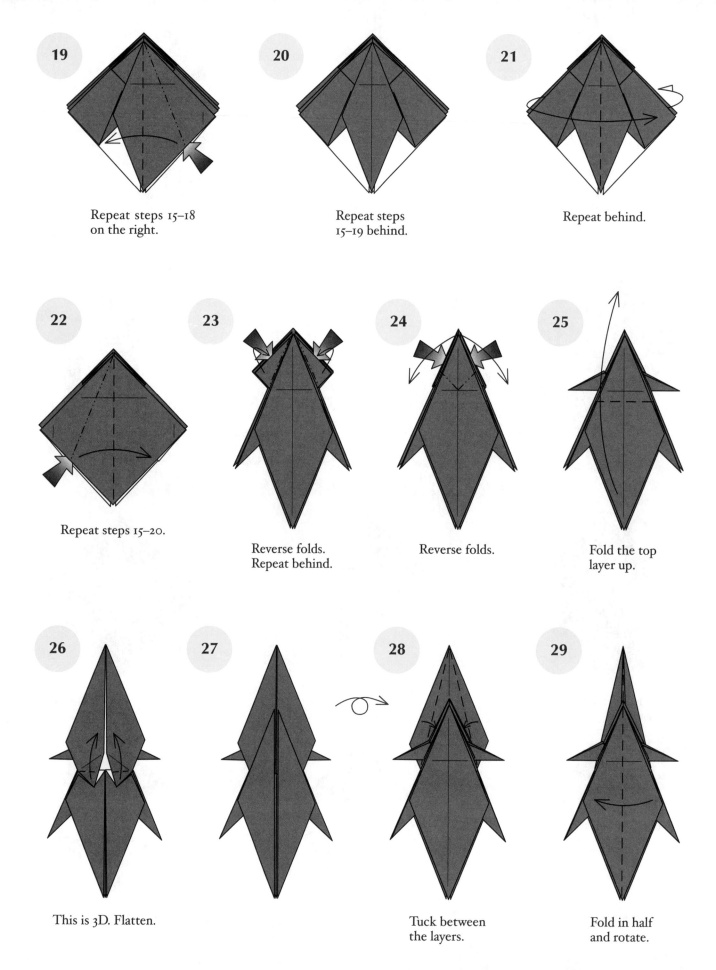

19 Repeat steps 15–18 on the right.

20 Repeat steps 15–19 behind.

21 Repeat behind.

22 Repeat steps 15–20.

23 Reverse folds. Repeat behind.

24 Reverse folds.

25 Fold the top layer up.

26 This is 3D. Flatten.

27

28 Tuck between the layers.

29 Fold in half and rotate.

30

This is a combination of squash folds. Repeat behind.

31

1

2

1. Spread a little bit to shape the wings, repeat behind.
2. Crimp-fold.

32

Double-rabbit-ear.

33

Reverse-fold.

34

Spread the head.

35

Reverse-fold.

36

Repeat steps 32–35 two times, but shape them differently.

37

4

1

2

3

1. Crimp folds.
2. Crimp-fold.
3. Crimp and reverse-fold.
4. Pleat folds.
Repeat behind.

38

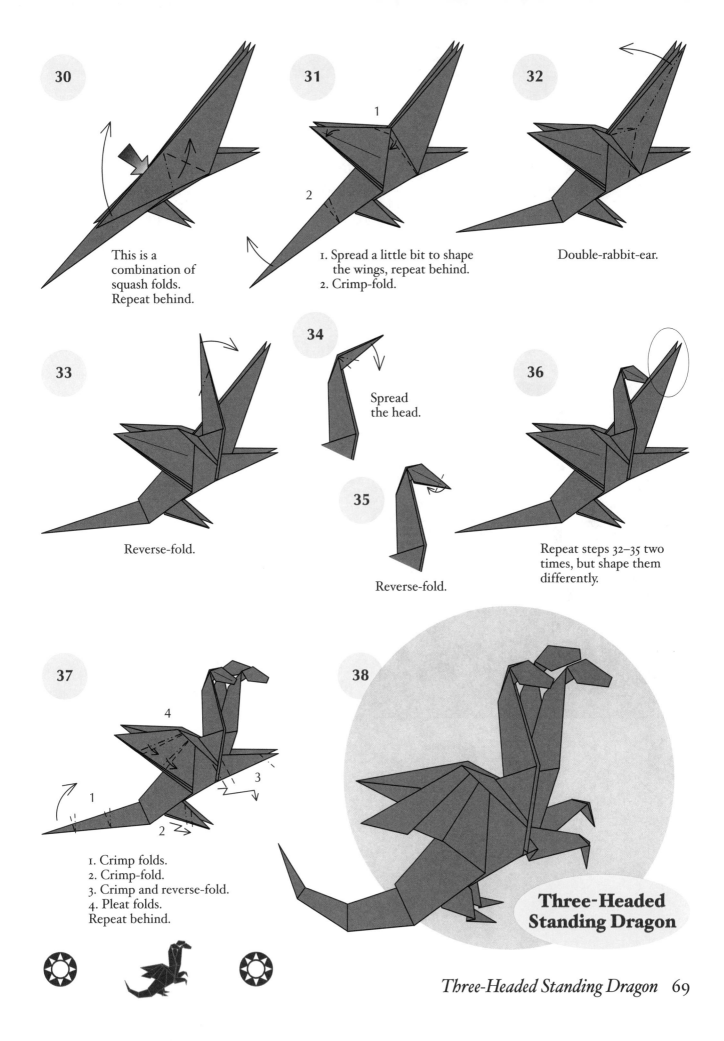

Three-Headed Standing Dragon

❋ Friend or Foe ❋

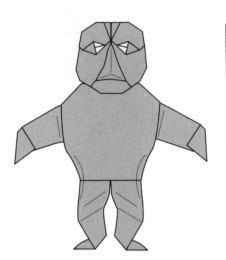

Throughout the land of the Enchanted Forest, your journey will take you to a Wizard, some Ogres, and Martian forms. Each can be either friendly or dangerous, so use your armaments wisely. If you are careful, you will gain new, unexpected powers.

Proceed when ready and may the Staff of Enchantment be at your side.

Wizard

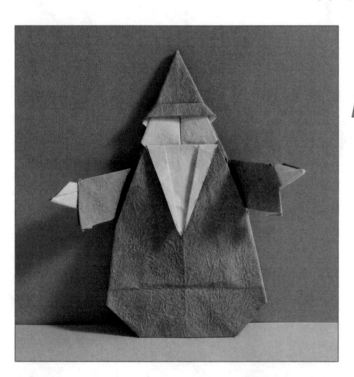

The wise Wizard uses the Sun, Moon, and stars to guide him through the tangled Enchanted Forest. He reads from magic scrolls and uses alchemy to heal wounded creatures.

The Wizard is expecting you with your staff and a few tamed dragons by your side. Offer him your staff to receive the magic potion. This gives you the power to make lightning, moonbeams, render claws and teeth harmless, and make small gems.

The Wizard will also welcome you without your staff or dragons. In that case, he will keep you safely in his abode as his new apprentice for 5,000 years.

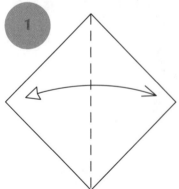

Fold and unfold.

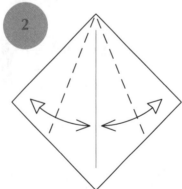

Kite-fold and unfold.

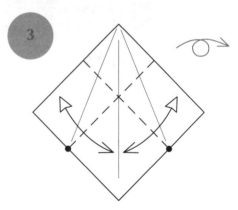

Fold and unfold.

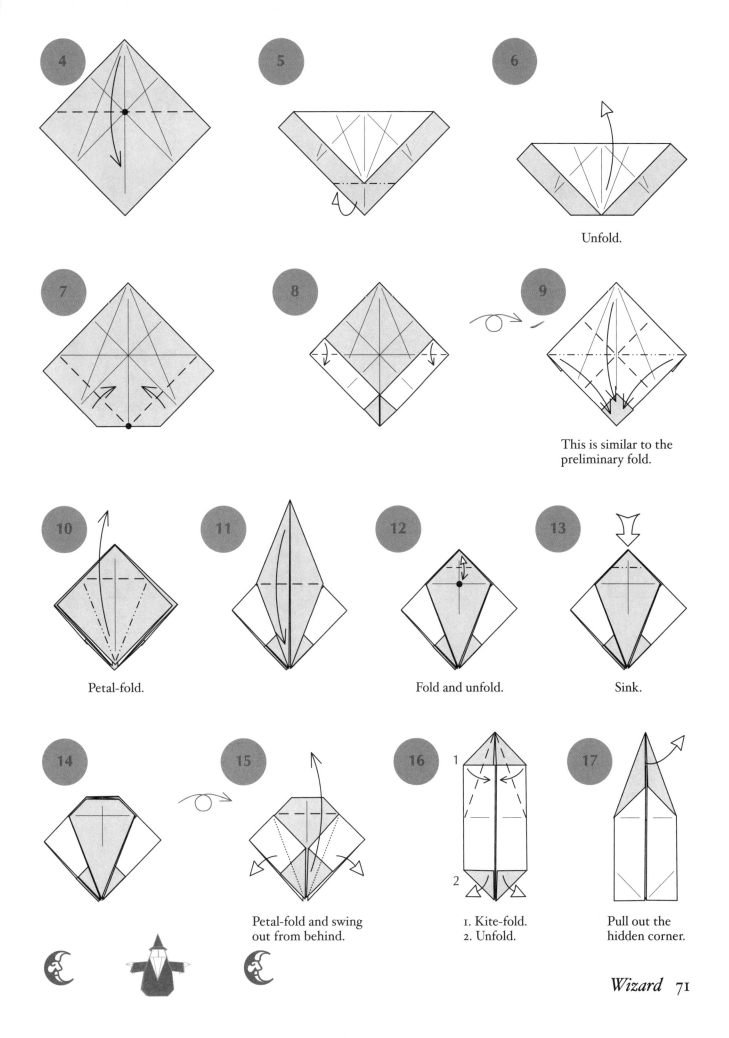

6

Unfold.

9

This is similar to the
preliminary fold.

10

Petal-fold.

12

Fold and unfold.

13

Sink.

15

Petal-fold and swing
out from behind.

16

1. Kite-fold.
2. Unfold.

17

Pull out the
hidden corner.

Wizard 71

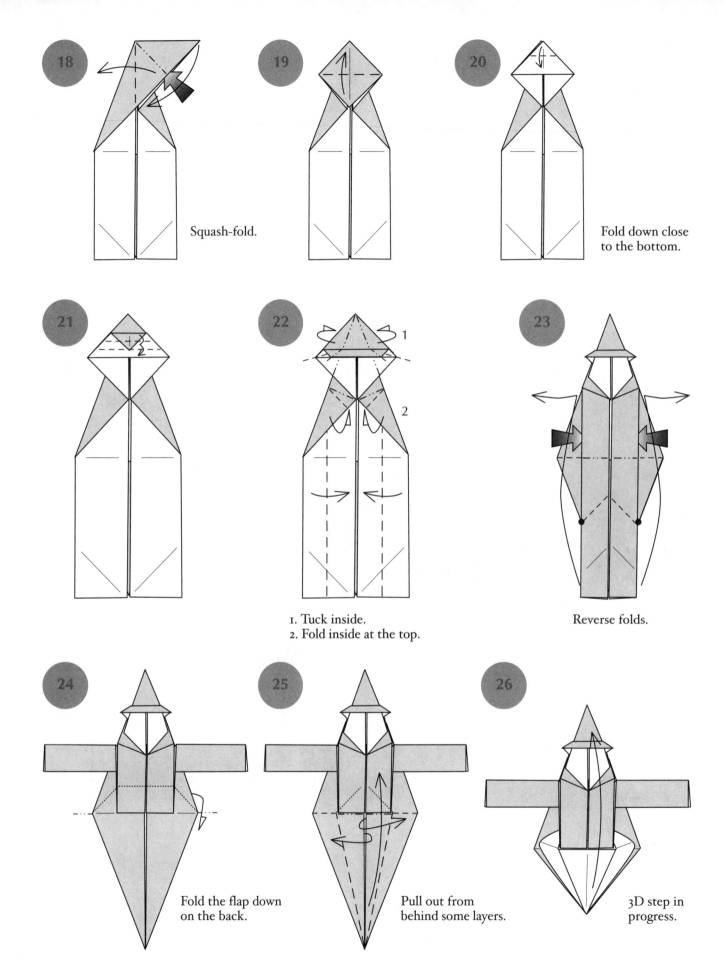

18

19 Squash-fold.

20 Fold down close to the bottom.

21

22
1. Tuck inside.
2. Fold inside at the top.

23 Reverse folds.

24 Fold the flap down on the back.

25 Pull out from behind some layers.

26 3D step in progress.

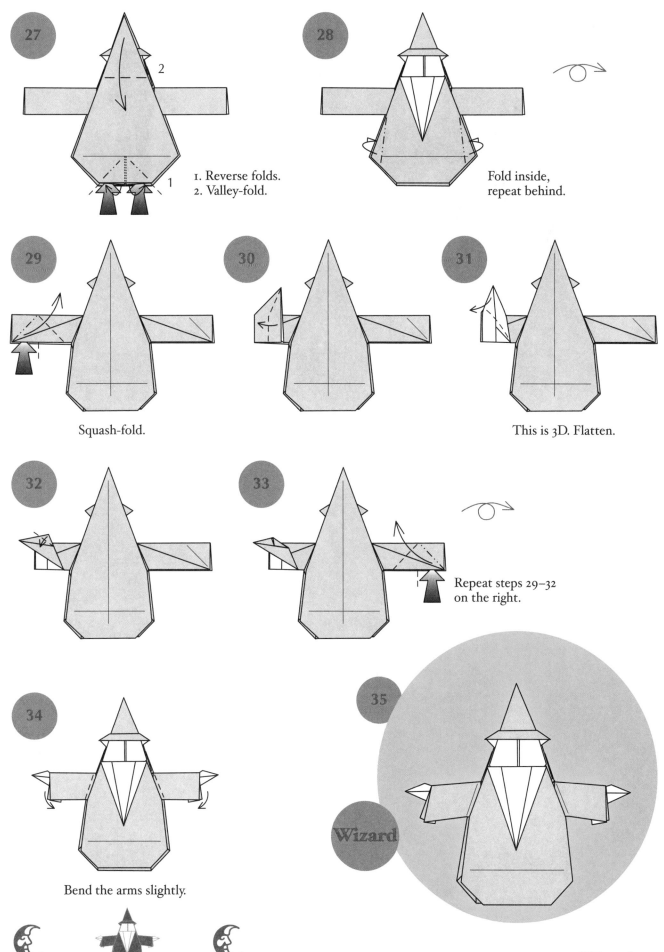

27

1. Reverse folds.
2. Valley-fold.

28

Fold inside,
repeat behind.

29

Squash-fold.

30

31

This is 3D. Flatten.

32

33

Repeat steps 29–32
on the right.

34

Bend the arms slightly.

35

Wizard

Ogre

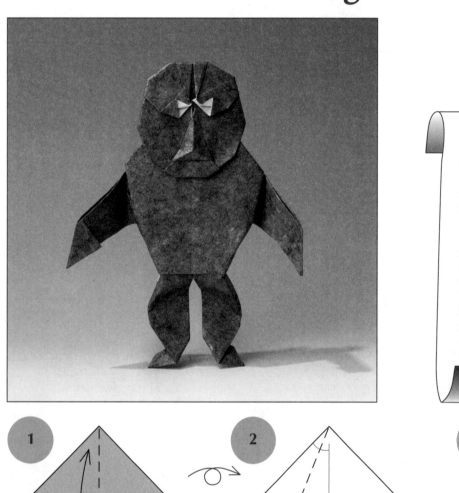

Ogres are not very friendly. They are interested in eating anything that moves. They will find you before you find them.

You will definitely need your shield and ax. If an Ogre approaches, display your ax while striking a menacing pose. The Ogre will not be interested in fighting and will offer its recent catch. However, if you see three or more Ogres, run and don't look back.

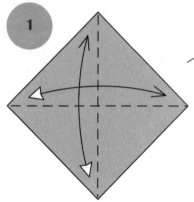

1

Fold and unfold.

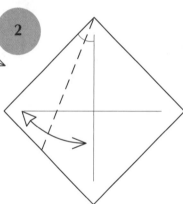

2

Fold and unfold.

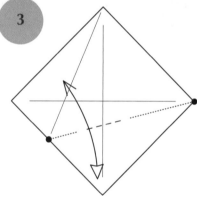

3

Fold and unfold on the diagonal.

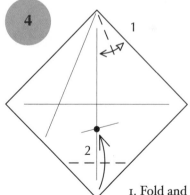

4

1. Fold and unfold.
2. Valley-fold.

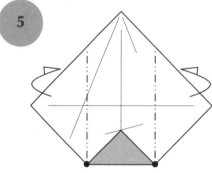

5

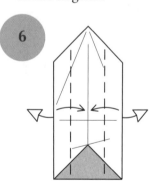

6

Fold to the center and swing out from behind.

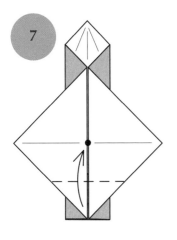

7

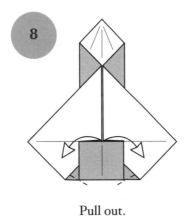

8

Pull out.

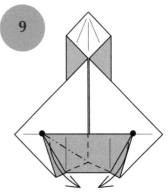

9

The dots will meet.

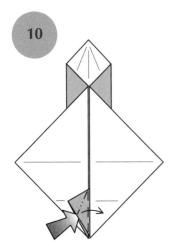

10

Squash-fold.

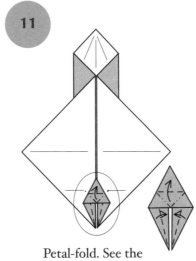

11

Petal-fold. See the
magnified view.

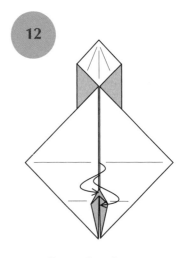

12

Bring the white
layers to the front.

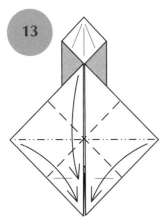

13

This is similar to the
preliminary fold.

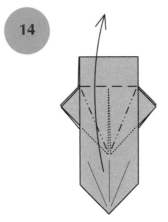

14

Petal-fold. Mountain-fold
along hidden creases.

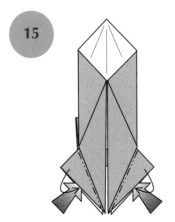

15

Reverse folds.

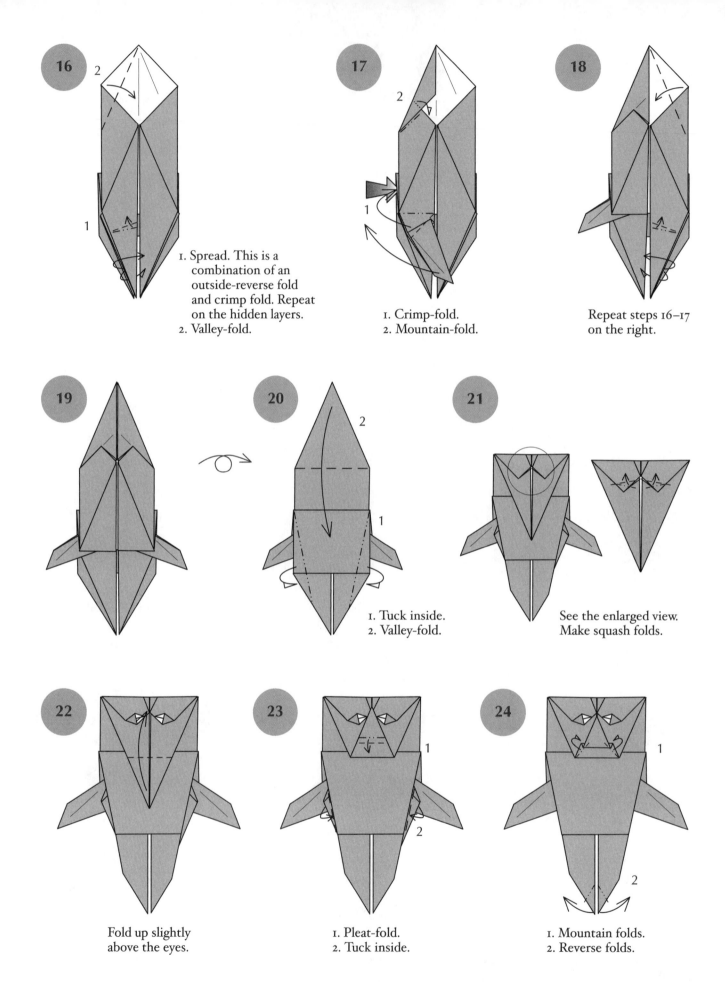

16

1. Spread. This is a combination of an outside-reverse fold and crimp fold. Repeat on the hidden layers.
2. Valley-fold.

17

1. Crimp-fold.
2. Mountain-fold.

18

Repeat steps 16–17 on the right.

19

20

1. Tuck inside.
2. Valley-fold.

21

See the enlarged view. Make squash folds.

22

Fold up slightly above the eyes.

23

1. Pleat-fold.
2. Tuck inside.

24

1. Mountain folds.
2. Reverse folds.

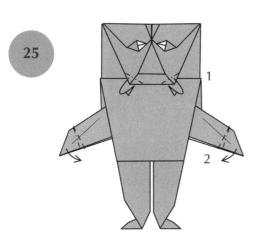

25

1. Mountain folds.
2. Crimp folds.

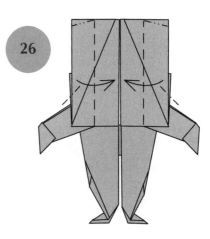

26

Fold to the center and make a few squash folds,

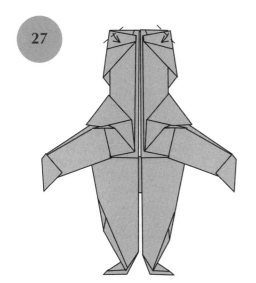

27

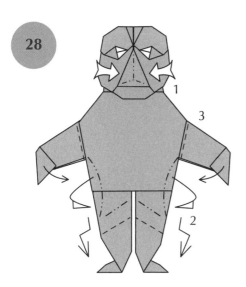

28

1. Make the nose 3D.
2. Shape the body and legs.
3. Bend the arms.

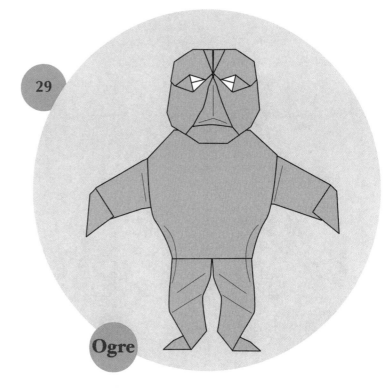

29

Ogre

Ogre 77

Martian

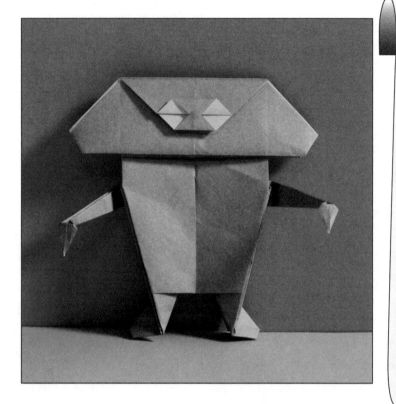

Martians found their way to the Enchanted Forest via Martian Meteorite Methods (methods beyond our understanding). Martians can change their shape and chemical composition at any time. They have a pair of special sensory organs, located on the extreme left and right sides of the head, that detect if they are being detected, even from light-years away. They will change their composition depending on who is detecting them. If they think someone from Earth is trying to find them, they transform into sand and rock.

Use your shield to hide yourself as you approach a Martian, but carry no weapon. Once you are close enough, the Martian will see there is nothing to fear, and give you the power so you, too, can change your shape. They will teach you Martianematics and the ways of Martiology. If you change to resemble another Martian, the Martian will take you to Mars and not leave your side for about 100,000 Martian years. You will know you are safe with them.

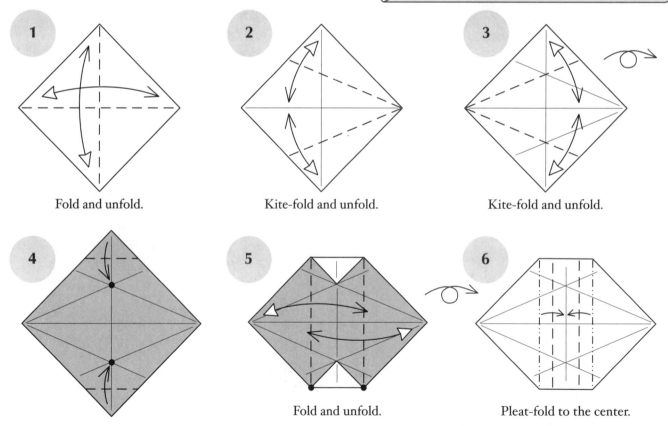

1 Fold and unfold.

2 Kite-fold and unfold.

3 Kite-fold and unfold.

4

5 Fold and unfold.

6 Pleat-fold to the center.

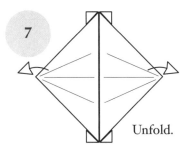

7

Unfold.

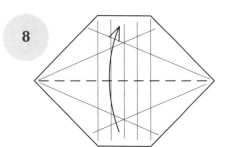

8

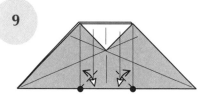

9

Fold and unfold.

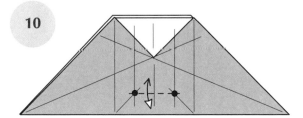

10

Fold and unfold.

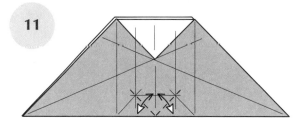

11

Fold and unfold.

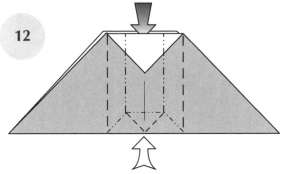

12

Collapse along the creases. Fold the same way in front and behind.

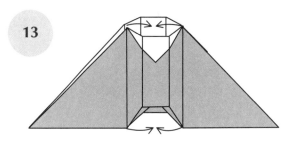

13

An intermediate 3D step.

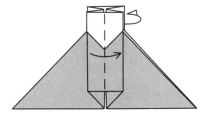

14

Repeat behind.

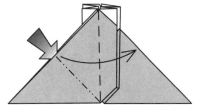

15

Squash-fold. Repeat behind.

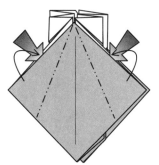

16

Reverse folds. Repeat behind.

Martian 79

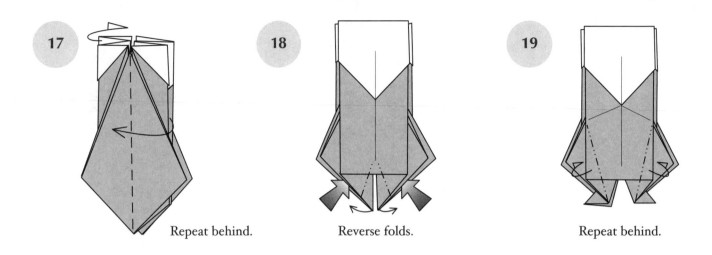

17 Repeat behind.

18 Reverse folds.

19 Repeat behind.

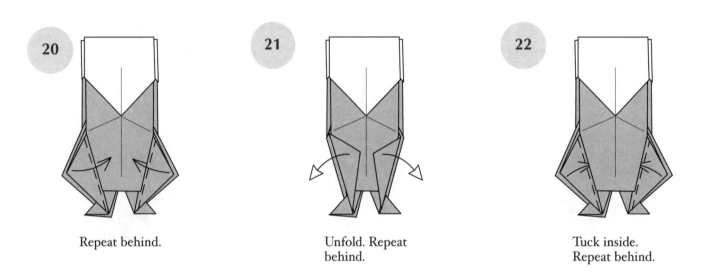

20 Repeat behind.

21 Unfold. Repeat behind.

22 Tuck inside. Repeat behind.

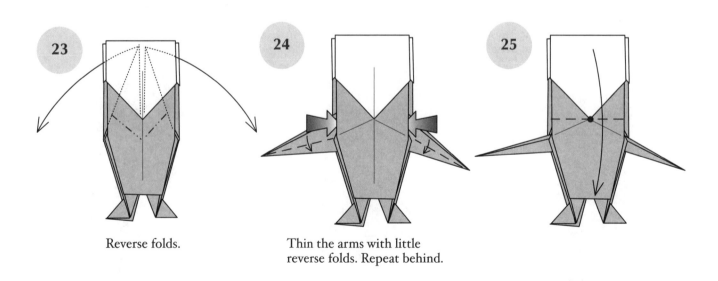

23 Reverse folds.

24 Thin the arms with little reverse folds. Repeat behind.

25

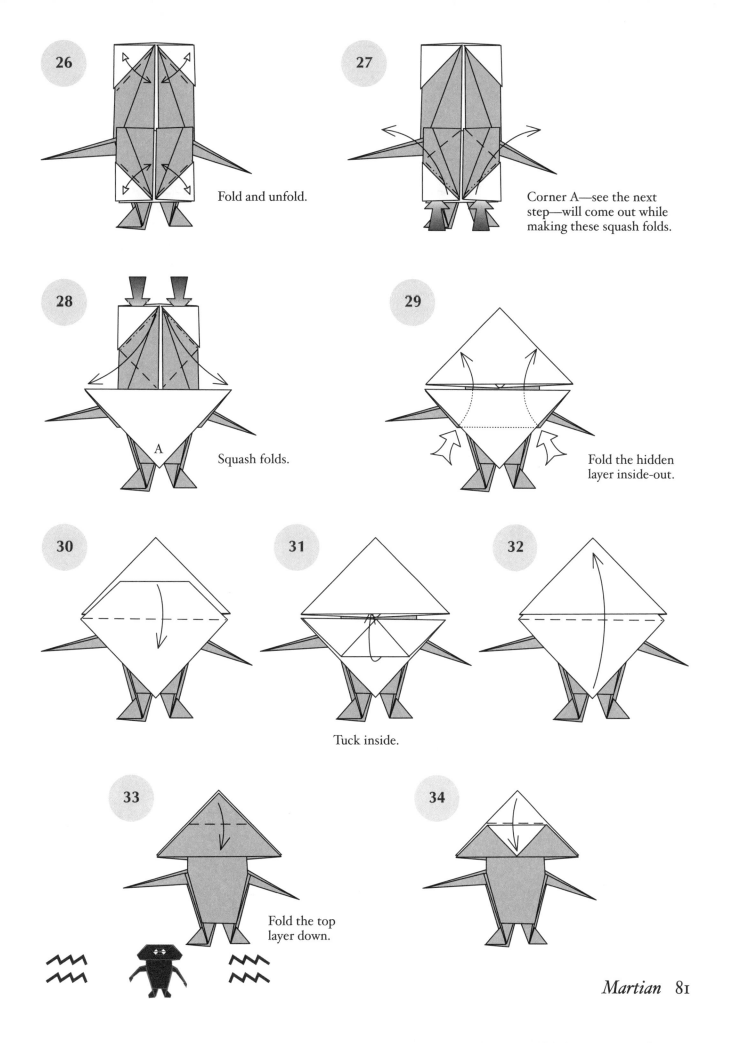

26   Fold and unfold.

27   Corner A—see the next step—will come out while making these squash folds.

28   Squash folds.

A

29   Fold the hidden layer inside-out.

30

31   Tuck inside.

32

33   Fold the top layer down.

34

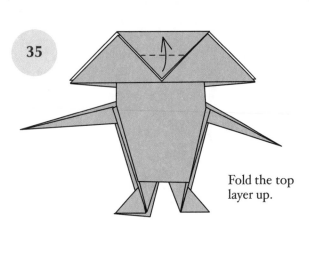

35

Fold the top layer up.

36

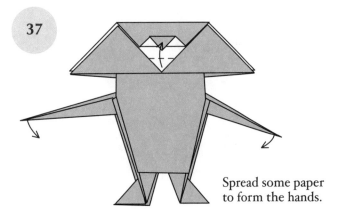

37

Spread some paper to form the hands.

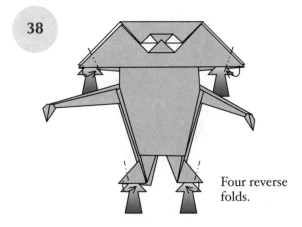

38

Four reverse folds.

39

Bend the arms. Adjust the feet so the Martian can stand.

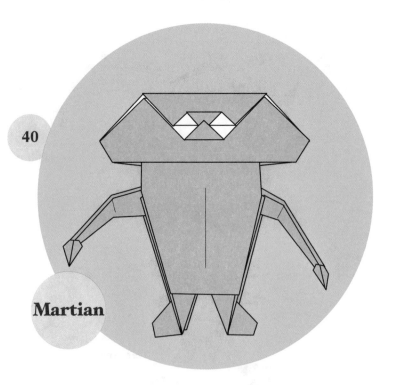

40

Martian

Two-Headed Martian

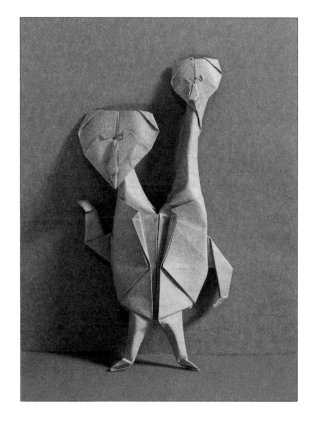

Martians evolved ages before life began on Earth. Through Martianetics, nature found it more efficient to have two heads, requiring half the food per head. This, among other advantages, allowed better survival during the Polar Ice Cap Age.

Due to their particular societal traditions, they do not recognize creatures with only one head. Turn your shield over to act as a mirror when approaching the Two-Headed Martian. Then recite "Lung-lung ga chooo-ga, oh chooo-ga" (greetings). The two heads will nod and you will receive the power to survive another Polar Ice Cap Age. However, be careful to say "...chooo-ga" and not "choo-ga" or you will be turned into a Polar Ice Cap.

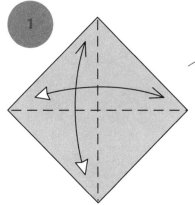

1 Fold and unfold.

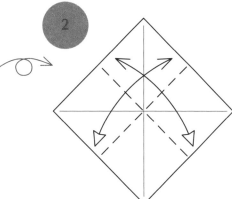

2 Fold and unfold.

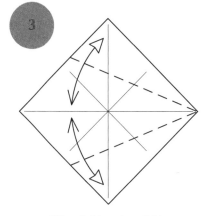

3 Kite-fold and unfold.

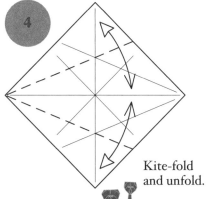

4 Kite-fold and unfold.

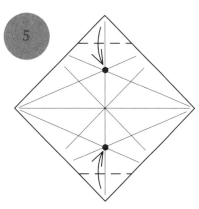

5

6 Fold and unfold.

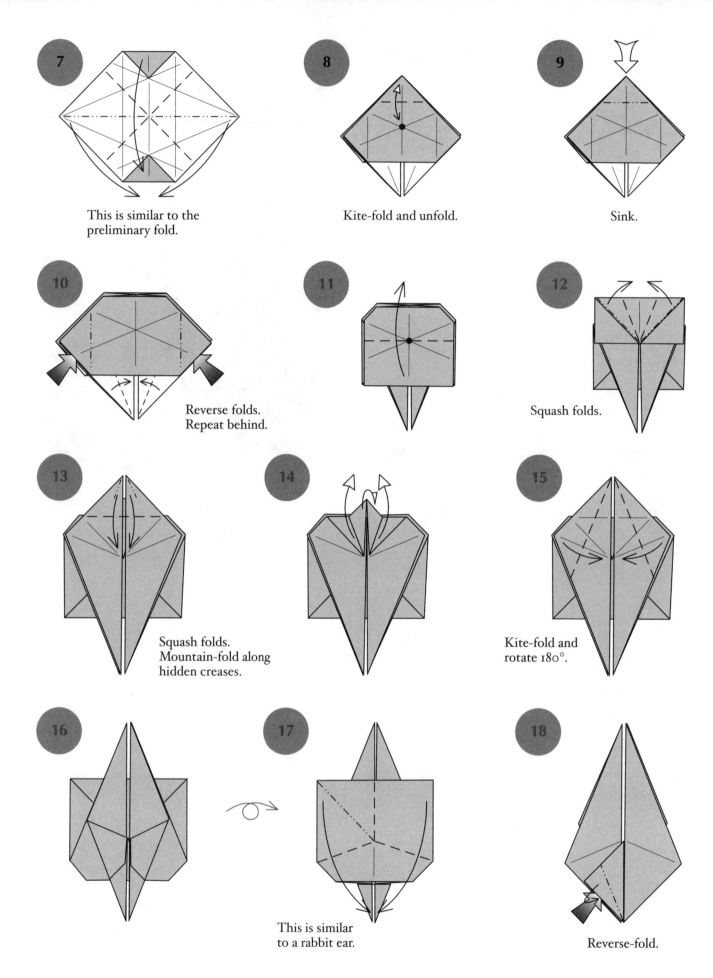

7 This is similar to the preliminary fold.

8 Kite-fold and unfold.

9 Sink.

10 Reverse folds. Repeat behind.

11

12 Squash folds.

13 Squash folds. Mountain-fold along hidden creases.

14

15 Kite-fold and rotate 180°.

16

17 This is similar to a rabbit ear.

18 Reverse-fold.

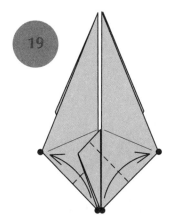

19

The pairs of
dots will meet.

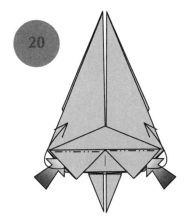

20

Reverse folds.

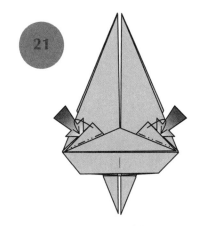

21

Reverse folds.

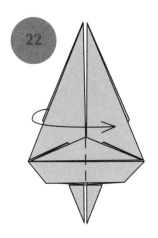

22

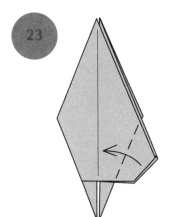

23

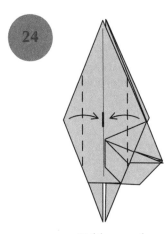

24

Fold towards
the center.

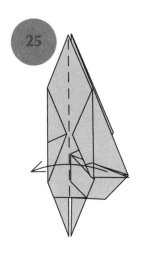

25

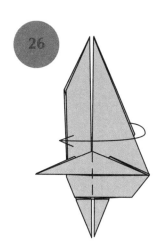

26

Repeat steps 22–25
on the right.

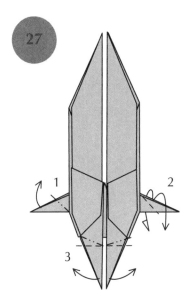

27

1. Reverse-fold.
2. Outside-reverse-fold.
3. Crimp folds.

Two-Headed Martian 85

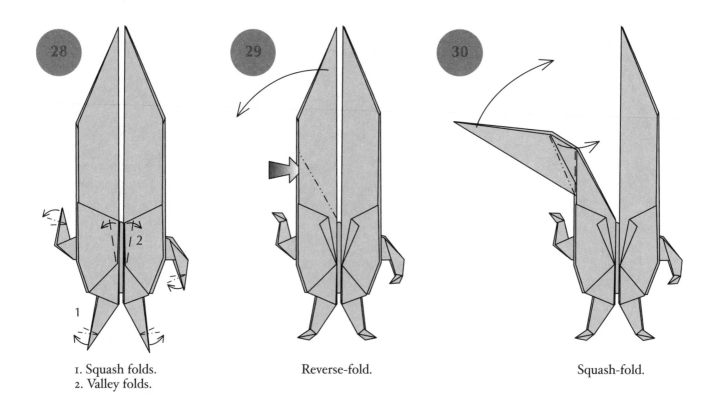

28

1. Squash folds.
2. Valley folds.

29

Reverse-fold.

30

Squash-fold.

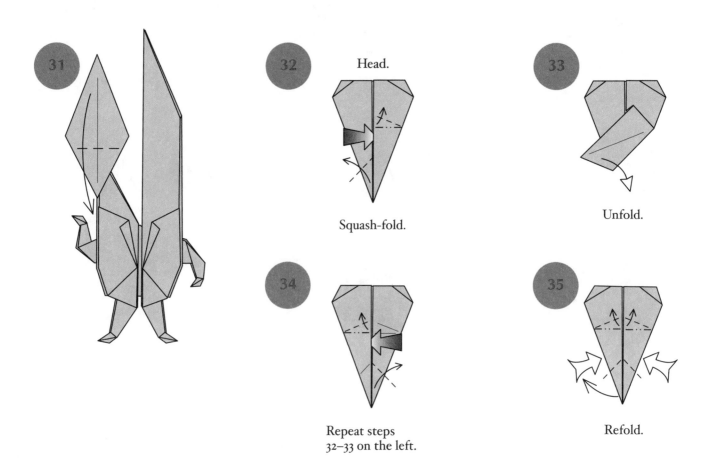

31

32

Head.

Squash-fold.

33

Unfold.

34

Repeat steps
32–33 on the left.

35

Refold.

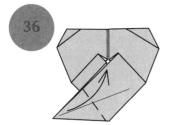
36

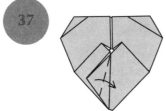
37

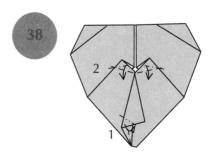
38

1. Shape the nose.
2. Squash folds.

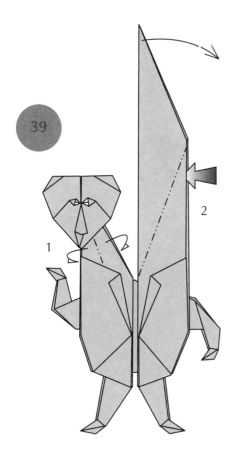
39

1. Shape the neck.
2. Repeat steps 29–39 on the right but with a taller neck and smaller head.

40

Two-Headed Martian

❁ Fantastic Creatures ❁

More adventures await. Throughout the Enchanted Forest, magical creatures are swimming, flying, protecting, and waiting. Each possess attributes for you to discover on your quest to become the Enchanted Master of Origami.

Be bold, be clever, but do not wait. Do not read any more of this or you will be stalling. There is nothing more to say other than: Begin!

Sea Serpent

The Sea Serpent is a huge sea monster. It attacks ships and gulps down people and other large animals. It can be found in the sea or in the moats that protect castles.

Fold a boat to attract the Serpent. When its head rises, use your staff to part the water. Out of water, the Serpent is powerless, and you can grab it by its neck and place it in your boat. The Sea Serpent will give you unlimited power to swim underwater in search of lost treasures.

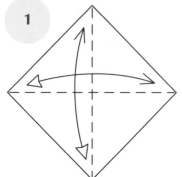

1

Fold and unfold.

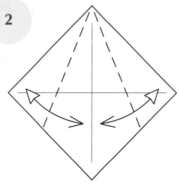

2

Kite-fold and unfold.

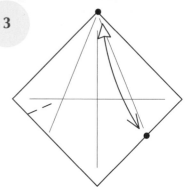

3

Fold and unfold by the edge.

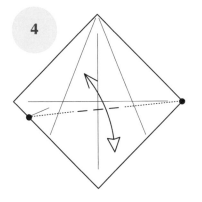

4

Fold and unfold by the diagonal.

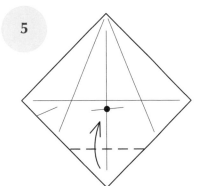

5

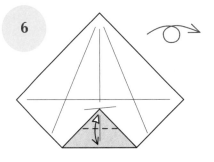

6

Fold and unfold.

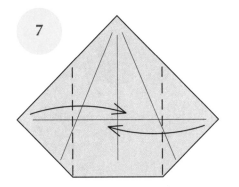

7

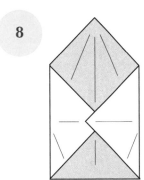

8

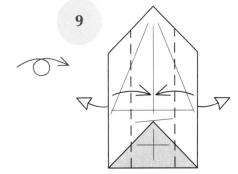

9

Fold to the center and swing out from behind.

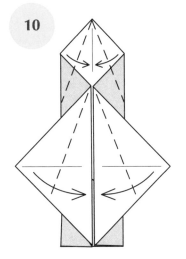

10

Kite folds.

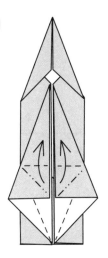

11

Squash folds.

12

Fold and unfold.

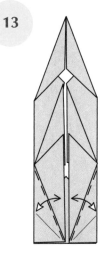

13

Fold and unfold.

Sea Serpent 89

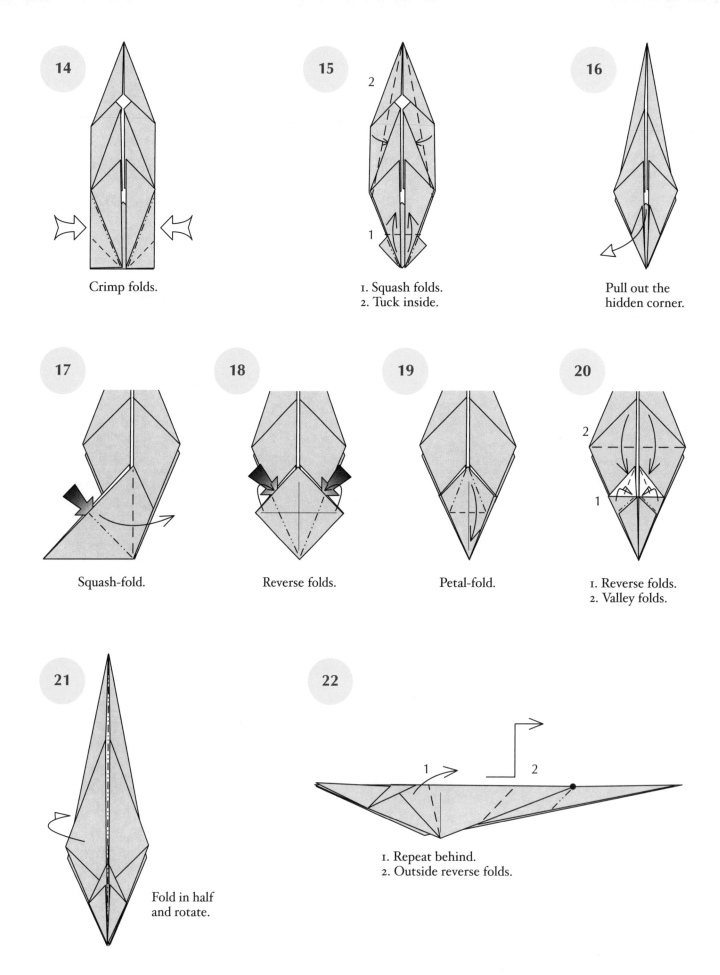

14

Crimp folds.

15

2

1

1. Squash folds.
2. Tuck inside.

16

Pull out the
hidden corner.

17

Squash-fold.

18

Reverse folds.

19

Petal-fold.

20

2

1

1. Reverse folds.
2. Valley folds.

21

Fold in half
and rotate.

22

1

2

1. Repeat behind.
2. Outside reverse folds.

23

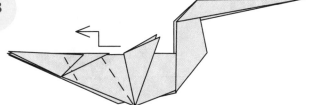

Outside reverse folds.

24

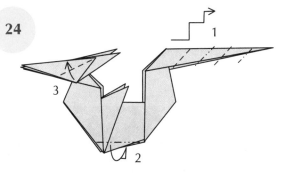

1. Outside reverse folds.
2. Repeat behind.
3. Repeat behind.

25

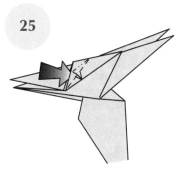

Spread-squash-fold,
repeat behind.

26

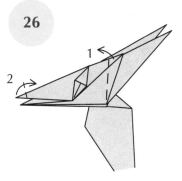

1. Repeat behind.
2. Outside-reverse-fold
   and spread.

27

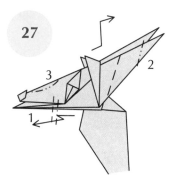

1. Crimp-fold.
2. Repeat behind.
3. Shape the head.

28

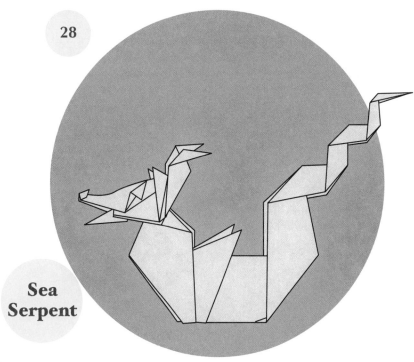

Sea Serpent

Griffin

The Griffin has the head of an eagle and body of a lion. This combines the king of birds with the king of beasts. The Griffin is majestic, powerful, courageous, and bold.

With its keen vision and sense of smell, the Griffin will find you as you wander through the Enchanted Forest. If the Wizard is with you, the Griffin will treat you as royalty. You will be adorned with gems, and at the top of your staff will appear a crystal ball that can locate more creatures. If the Wizard is not with you when the Griffin finds you, you will have to sing for your safety.

1

Fold and unfold.

2

Kite-fold and unfold.

3

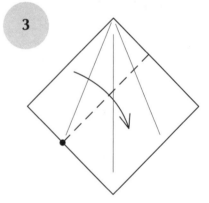

4

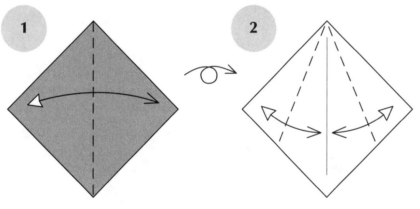

5

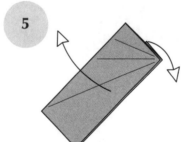

Unfold.

6

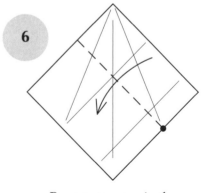

Repeat steps 3–4 in the opposite direction.

7

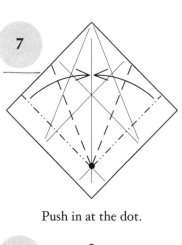

Push in at the dot.

8

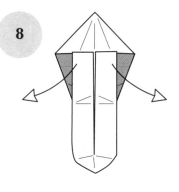

Unfold.

9

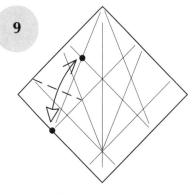

Fold and unfold.

10

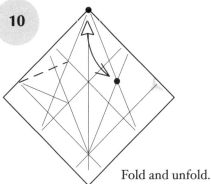

Fold and unfold.

11

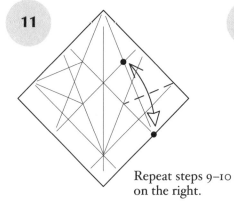

Repeat steps 9–10 on the right.

12

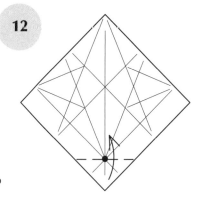

13

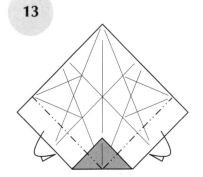

14

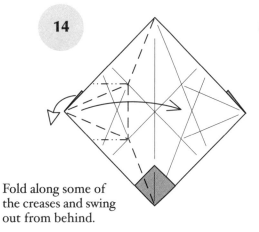

Fold along some of the creases and swing out from behind.

15

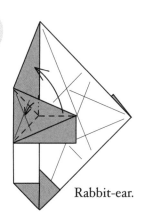

Rabbit-ear.

16

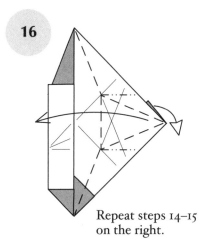

Repeat steps 14–15 on the right.

17

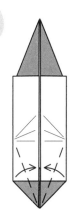

18

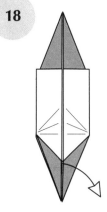

Pull out the hidden corner.

19

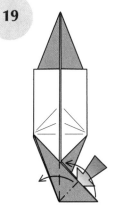

Squash-fold.

Griffin 93

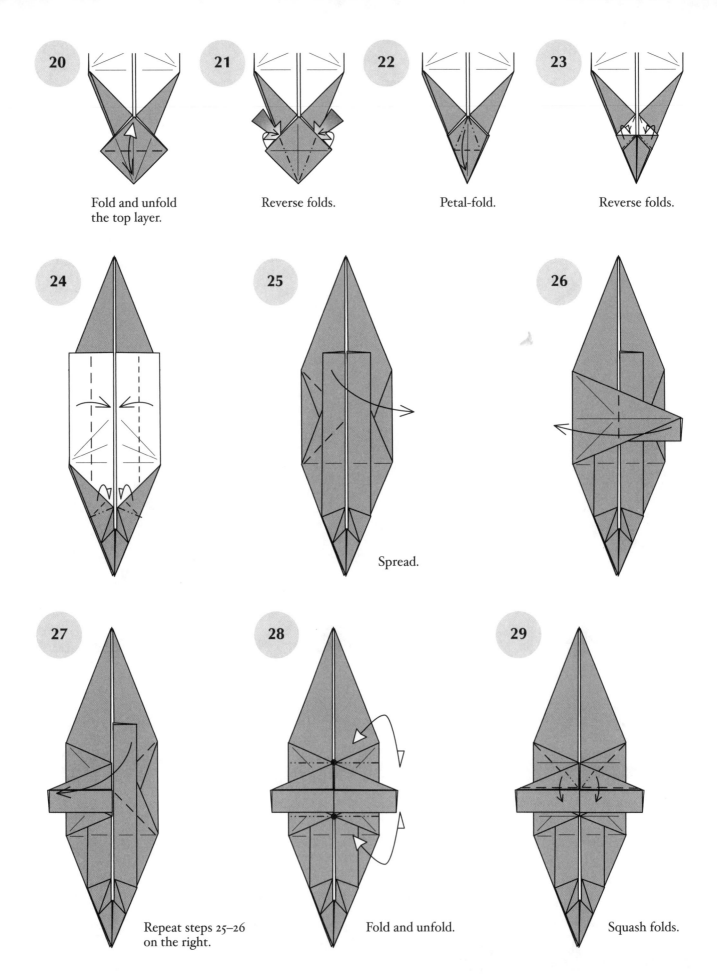

20 Fold and unfold the top layer.

21 Reverse folds.

22 Petal-fold.

23 Reverse folds.

25 Spread.

27 Repeat steps 25–26 on the right.

28 Fold and unfold.

29 Squash folds.

Dragons and Other Fantastic Creatures in Origami

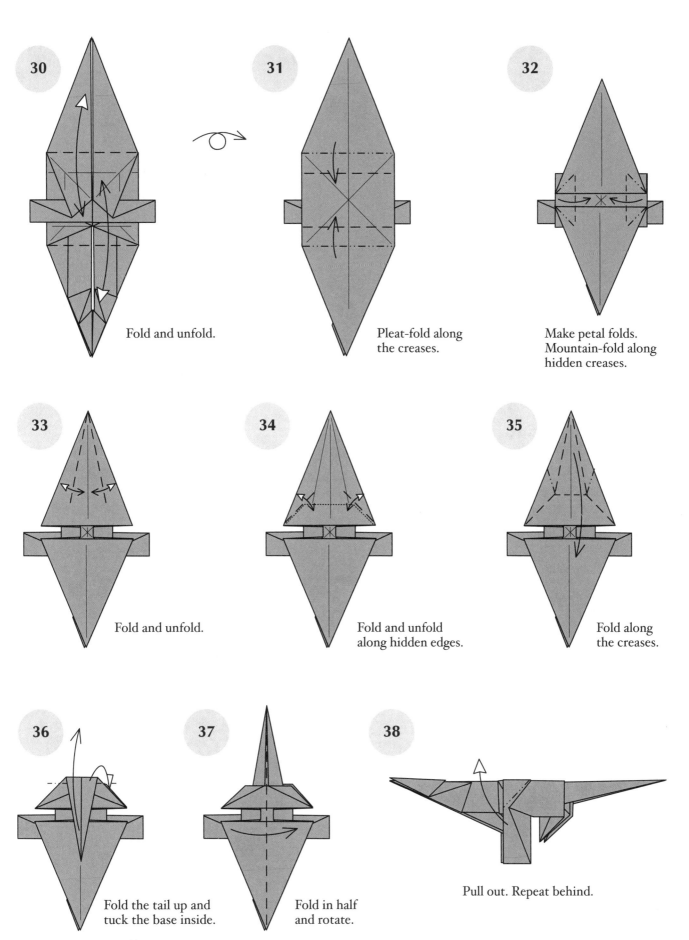

30 Fold and unfold.

31 Pleat-fold along the creases.

32 Make petal folds. Mountain-fold along hidden creases.

33 Fold and unfold.

34 Fold and unfold along hidden edges.

35 Fold along the creases.

36 Fold the tail up and tuck the base inside.

37 Fold in half and rotate.

38 Pull out. Repeat behind.

Griffin 95

39

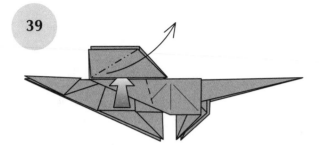

Squash-fold. Repeat behind.

40

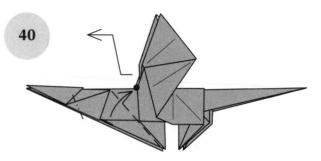

Outside-reverse folds.

41

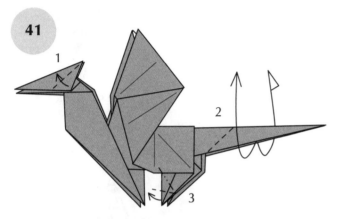

1. Repeat behind.
2. Outside-reverse-fold.
3. Crimp-fold, repeat behind.

42

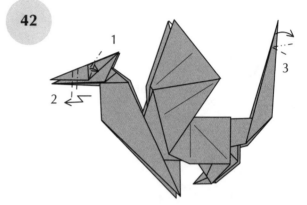

1. Squash-fold, repeat behind.
2. Crimp-fold.
3. Spread the tip of the tail.

43

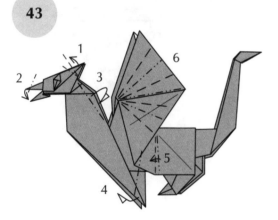

1. Pleat-fold.
2. Reverse-fold.
3. Fold inside.
4. Mountain-fold all the layers.
5. Crimp-fold.
6. Pleat-fold.
Repeat behind.

44

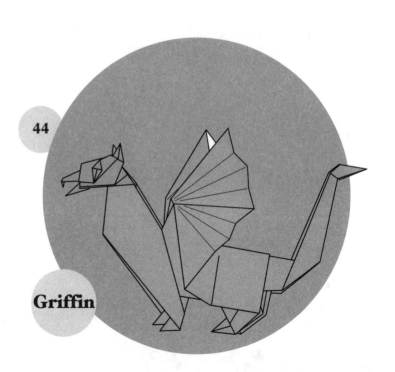

Griffin

Winged Lion

The Winged Lion is king over its surroundings. It will protect small creatures nearby and threaten intruders.

Attempting to battle with your armaments will do no good. Approach with your staff, Two-Headed Dragon, and Two-Headed Martian. The Winged Lion will recognize your bravery and will offer you the Crown of Strength, necessary for your continued survival in the Enchanted Forest.

1

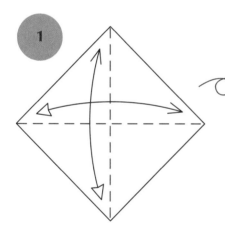

Fold and unfold.

2

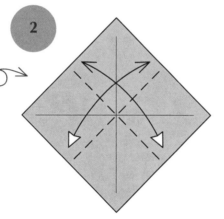

Fold and unfold.

3

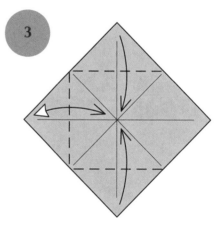

Fold and unfold on the left.

4

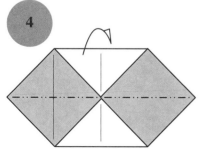

5

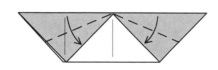

6

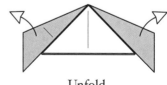

Unfold.

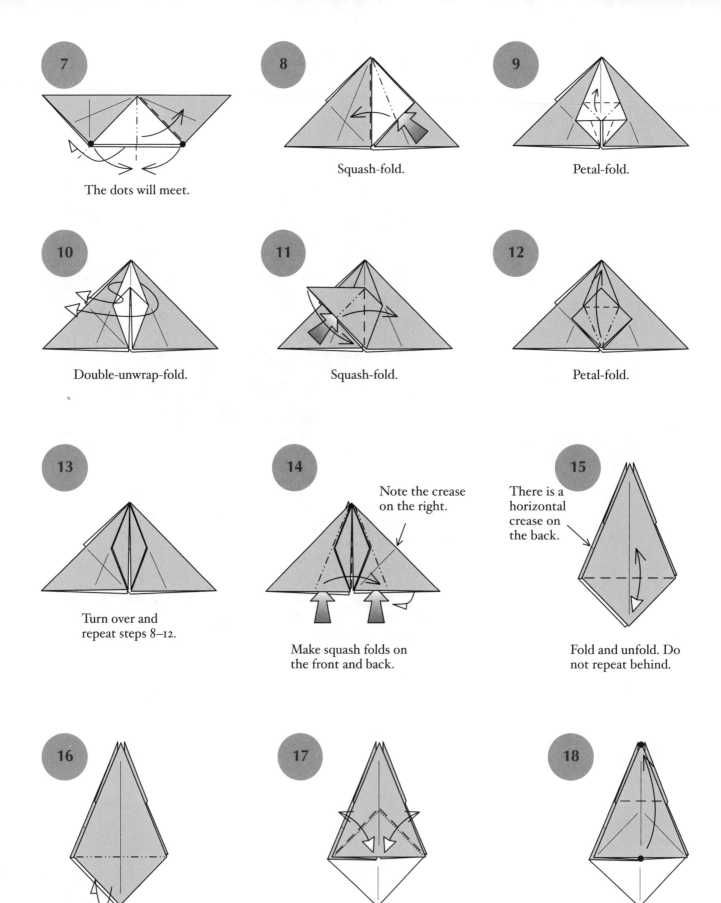

7 The dots will meet.

8 Squash-fold.

9 Petal-fold.

10 Double-unwrap-fold.

11 Squash-fold.

12 Petal-fold.

13 Turn over and repeat steps 8–12.

14 Note the crease on the right.

Make squash folds on the front and back.

15 There is a horizontal crease on the back.

Fold and unfold. Do not repeat behind.

16 Tuck inside.

17 Fold and unfold the top layer along the hidden edge.

18

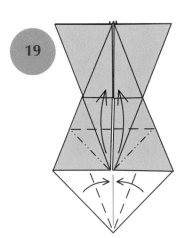

19

Squash folds.

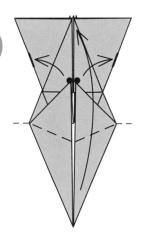

20

Slide the dots to the edge. Valley-fold along the creases.

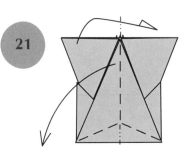

21

Lift the neck up while folding in half. Rotate.

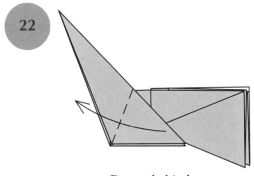

22

Repeat behind.

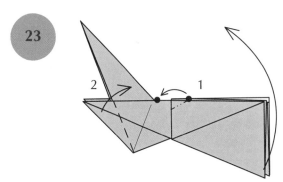

23

1. Slide the wings.
2. Valley-fold.
Repeat behind.

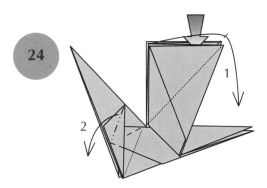

24

1. Reverse-fold the center layers along hidden creases.
2. Squash-fold, repeat behind.

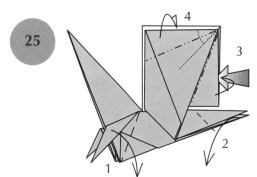

25

1. Valley-fold.
2. Valley-fold.
3. Reverse-fold.
4. Mountain-fold to the hidden edge.
Repeat behind.

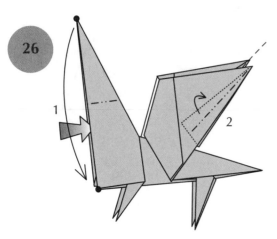

26

1. Reverse-fold.
2. Reverse-fold a thin flap
   between the wings.

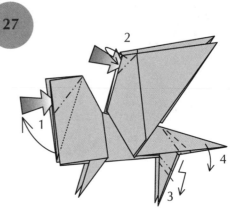

27

1. Reverse-fold.
2. Reverse-fold, repeat behind.
3. Crimp-fold, repeat behind.
4. Crimp-fold.

28

1. Crimp-fold.
2. Reverse-fold.
3. Repeat behind.
4. Squash-fold, repeat behind.
5. Crimp-fold, repeat behind.
6. Repeat behind.
7. Pleat folds, repeat behind.

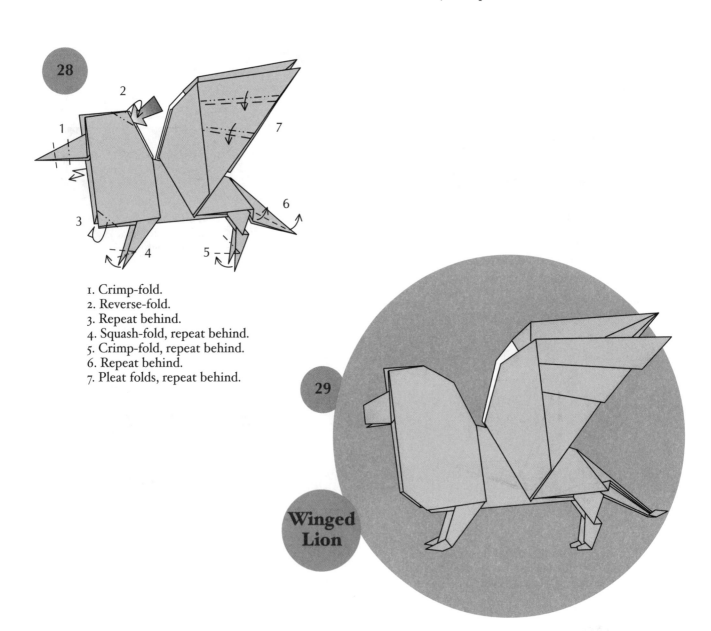

29

**Winged
Lion**

Winged Wolf

The Winged Wolf is a free, spirited, devious, wild animal, always searching for its next meal. It claims its territory by howling at the moon.

To overpower the Winged Wolf, wear the Crown of Strength and ride on the back of the Three-Headed Standing Dragon with your staff. The Winged Wolf will give you the power to tame other wild animals. By offering your staff, you will also learn how to howl at the moon.

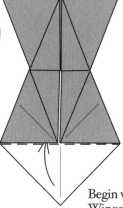

Begin with step 19 of the Winged Lion (page 97). Tuck inside.

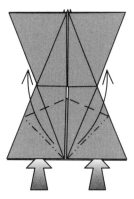

Squash folds.

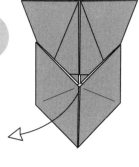

Pull out the hidden corner.

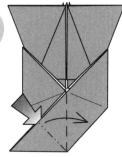

Squash-fold.

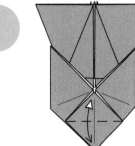

Fold and unfold.

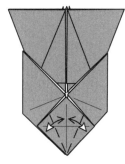

Fold and unfold.

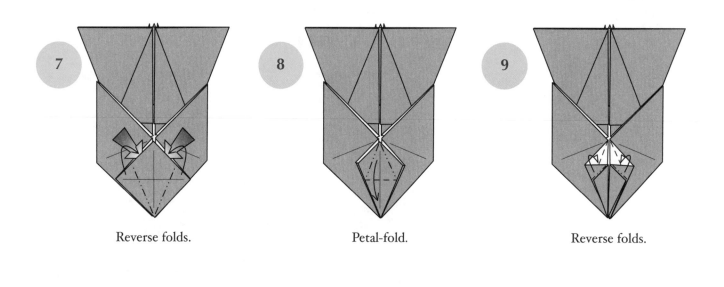

7 Reverse folds.

8 Petal-fold.

9 Reverse folds.

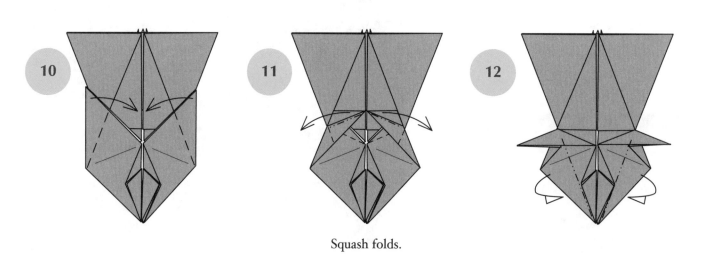

10

11 Squash folds.

12

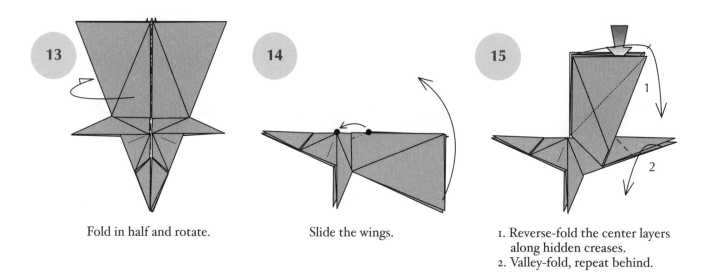

13 Fold in half and rotate.

14 Slide the wings.

15
1. Reverse-fold the center layers along hidden creases.
2. Valley-fold, repeat behind.

16

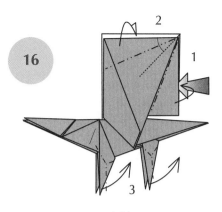

1. Reverse-fold.
2. Mountain-fold to the hidden edge.
3. Double-rabbit-ear the legs, repeat behind.

17

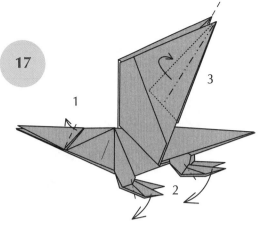

1. Repeat behind.
2. Reverse folds, repeat behind.
3. Reverse-fold a thin flap between the wings.

18

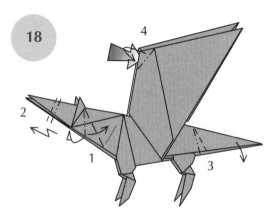

1. Crimp-fold.
2. Crimp-fold.
3. Crimp-fold.
4. Reverse-fold, repeat behind.

19

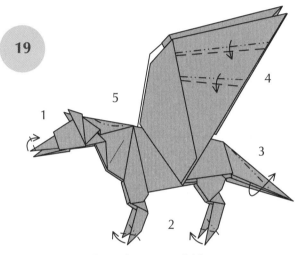

1. Outside-reverse-fold.
2. Crimp folds, repeat behind.
3. Spread, repeat behind.
4. Pleat folds, repeat behind.
5. Shape the neck.

20

Winged Wolf

Pegasus

Pegasus is the noble, winged horse representing power, speed, wisdom, fame, poetry, and inspiration. Raise your staff high over your head and Pegasus will come. Pegasus will take you anywhere throughout the Enchanted Forest. Upon receiving his ride, you will be inspired to write poetry and create new origami creatures.

1

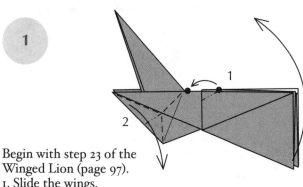

Begin with step 23 of the Winged Lion (page 97).
1. Slide the wings.
2. Rabbit-ear.
Repeat behind.

2

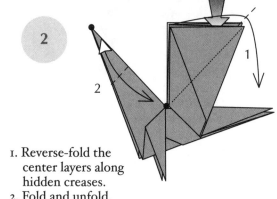

1. Reverse-fold the center layers along hidden creases.
2. Fold and unfold.

3

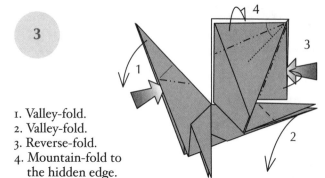

1. Valley-fold.
2. Valley-fold.
3. Reverse-fold.
4. Mountain-fold to the hidden edge.
Repeat behind.

4

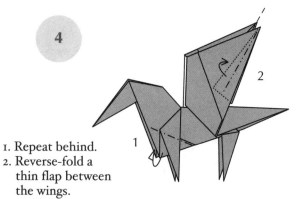

1. Repeat behind.
2. Reverse-fold a thin flap between the wings.

5

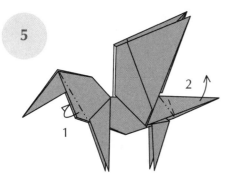

1. Repeat behind.
2. Crimp-fold.

6

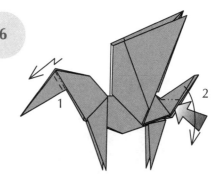

1. Crimp-fold.
2. Reverse-fold.

7

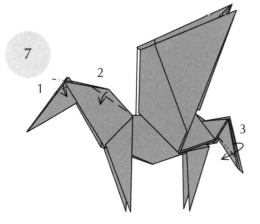

1. Repeat behind.
2. Valley-fold.
3. Spread, repeat behind.

8

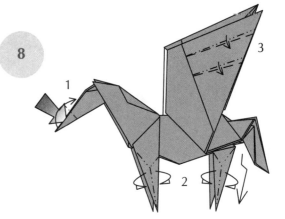

1. Reverse-fold.
2. Thin and shape the legs, repeat behind.
3. Pleat folds, repeat behind.

9

Pegasus

Unicorn

The Unicorn lives in the highest realm of thought. It is a creature of Perfection and its horn has magical healing powers. It is a symbol of mystery and childhood.

The Unicorn is secretly protecting you throughout your visit in the Enchanted Forest. If you have traveled unscathed this far, it is only because of the Unicorn. Simply thank the Unicorn; turn around, and it will be standing there. Touch its horn and it will grant you access to the highest realms of thought.

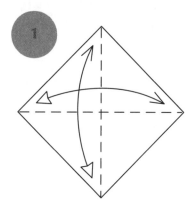

Fold and unfold.

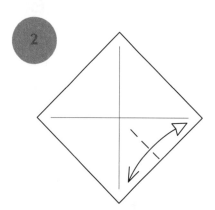

Fold and unfold in the bottom half.

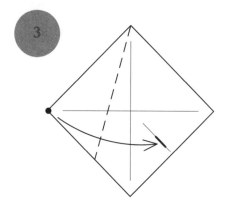

Bring the corner to the line.

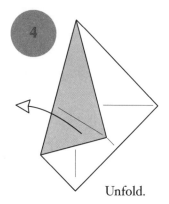

Unfold.

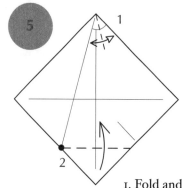

1. Fold and unfold.
2. Valley-fold.

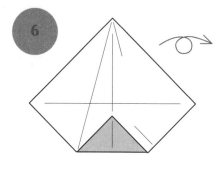

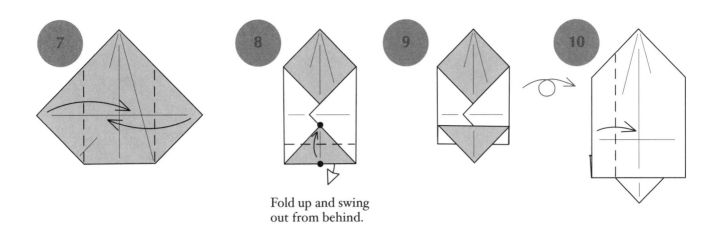

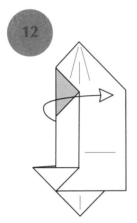

Fold up and swing
out from behind.

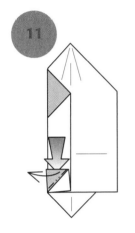

Squash-fold.

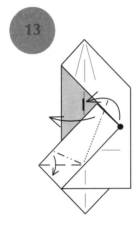

Pull out.

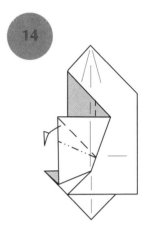

Squash-fold.

Squash-fold.

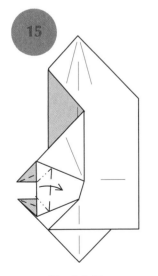

Petal-fold.

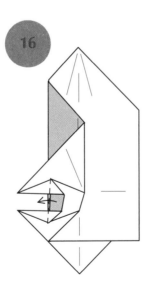

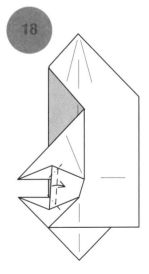

Fold inside.

Spread squash folds.

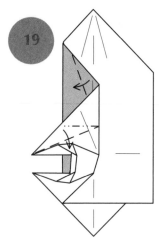

19

Squash-fold.

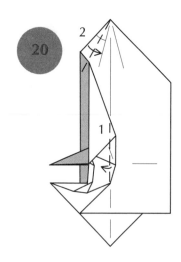

20

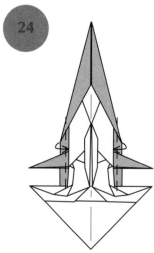

21

Repeat steps 10–20
on the right.

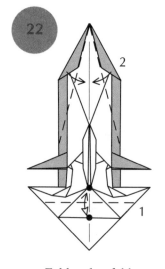

22

1. Fold and unfold.
2. Fold along creases
   at the top.

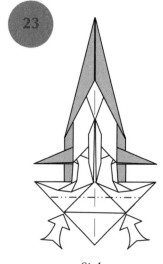

23

Sink.

24

Fold thin strips.

25

Fold and unfold.

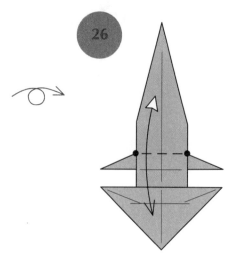

26

Fold and unfold.

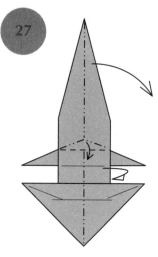

27

Fold the neck up while
folding in half. Rotate.

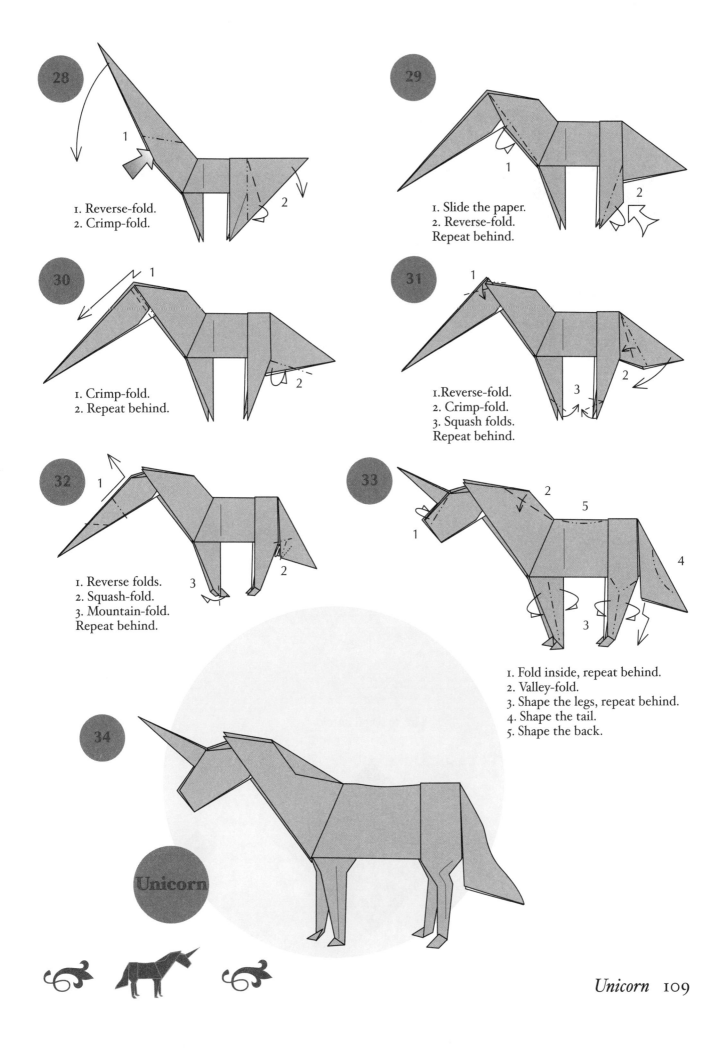

28

1. Reverse-fold.
2. Crimp-fold.

29

1. Slide the paper.
2. Reverse-fold.
Repeat behind.

30

1. Crimp-fold.
2. Repeat behind.

31

1. Reverse-fold.
2. Crimp-fold.
3. Squash folds.
Repeat behind.

32

1. Reverse folds.
2. Squash-fold.
3. Mountain-fold.
Repeat behind.

33

1. Fold inside, repeat behind.
2. Valley-fold.
3. Shape the legs, repeat behind.
4. Shape the tail.
5. Shape the back.

34

Unicorn

Phoenix

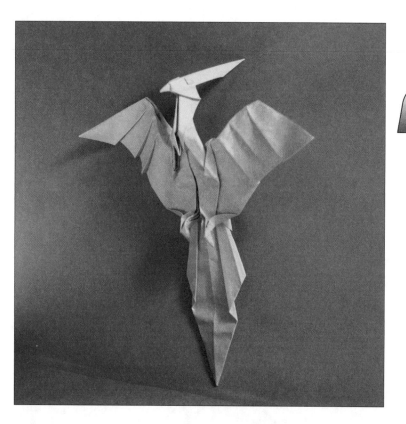

The Phoenix is often depicted as a purple bird with a long life which cycles through transformations. When ready, it will give up its old self and emerge through fire and ashes to be reborn on a higher realm. This relates to the way the Sun emerges every morning in a ball of fire. The Phoenix symbolizes time, magic, rebirth, creativity, transformation, and eternal youth.

Patience is required to find the Phoenix. At the most unexpected time, a fire will appear and the Phoenix will rise out of it. Upon viewing this, you will have the power of all its symbols and ready to begin a new chapter in your life, just as every day we begin again.

1

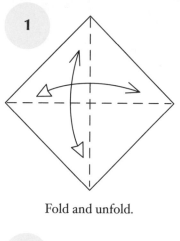

Fold and unfold.

2

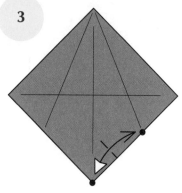

Kite-fold and unfold.

3

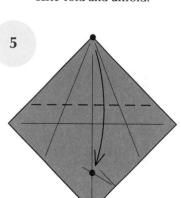

Fold and unfold by the edge.

4

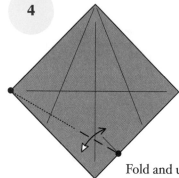

Fold and unfold by the diagonal.

5

6

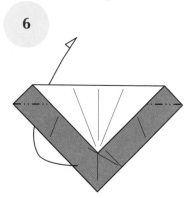

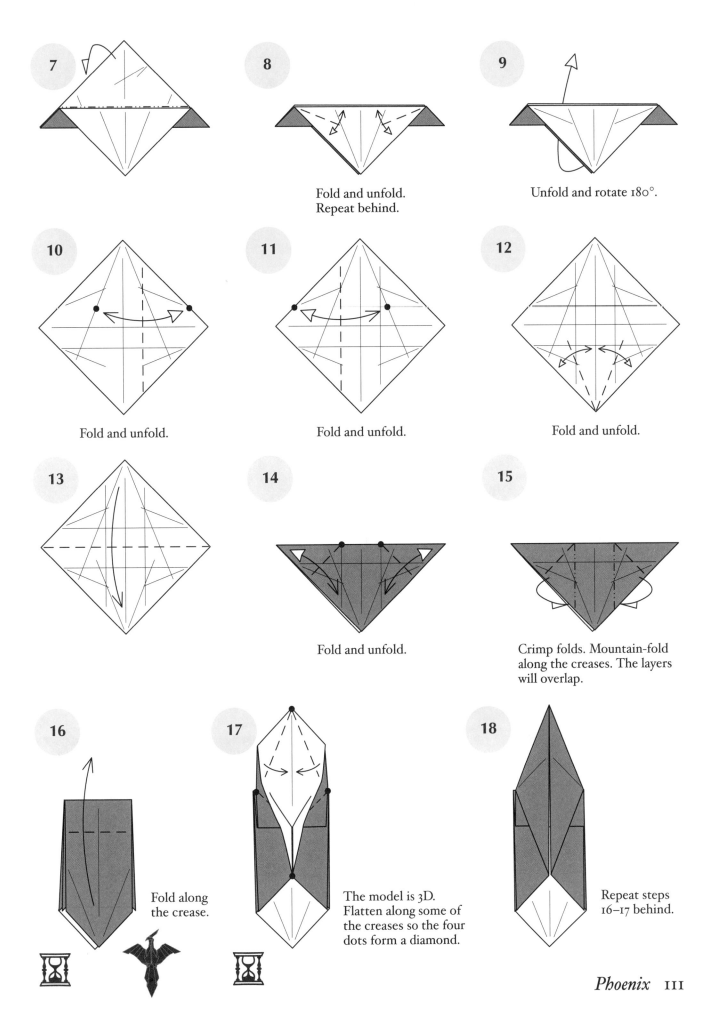

7

8

Fold and unfold.
Repeat behind.

9

Unfold and rotate 180°.

10

Fold and unfold.

11

Fold and unfold.

12

Fold and unfold.

13

14

Fold and unfold.

15

Crimp folds. Mountain-fold
along the creases. The layers
will overlap.

16

Fold along
the crease.

17

The model is 3D.
Flatten along some of
the creases so the four
dots form a diamond.

18

Repeat steps
16–17 behind.

Phoenix 111

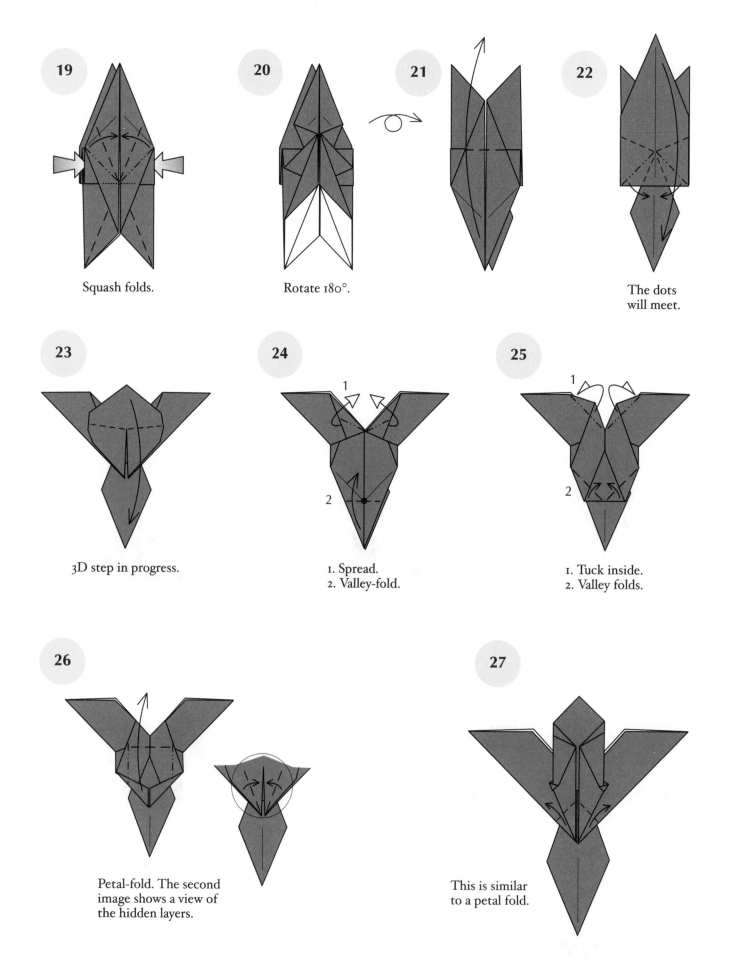

19

Squash folds.

20

Rotate 180°.

21

22

The dots
will meet.

23

3D step in progress.

24

1. Spread.
2. Valley-fold.

25

1. Tuck inside.
2. Valley folds.

26

Petal-fold. The second
image shows a view of
the hidden layers.

27

This is similar
to a petal fold.

28

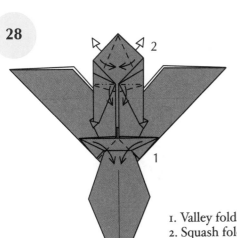

1. Valley folds.
2. Squash folds and swing out from behind.

29

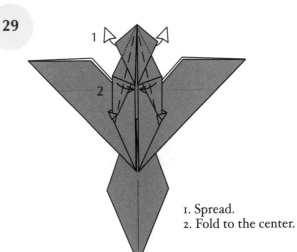

1. Spread.
2. Fold to the center.

30

31

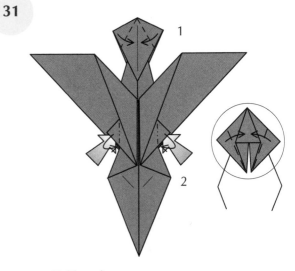

1. Fold to the center.
2. Reverse folds. The second image shows a view of the hidden layers.

32

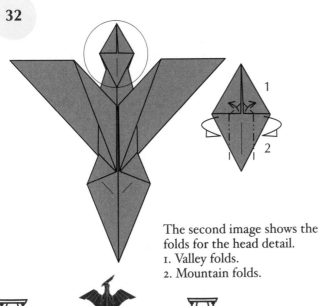

The second image shows the folds for the head detail.
1. Valley folds.
2. Mountain folds.

33

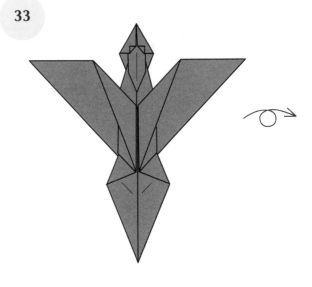

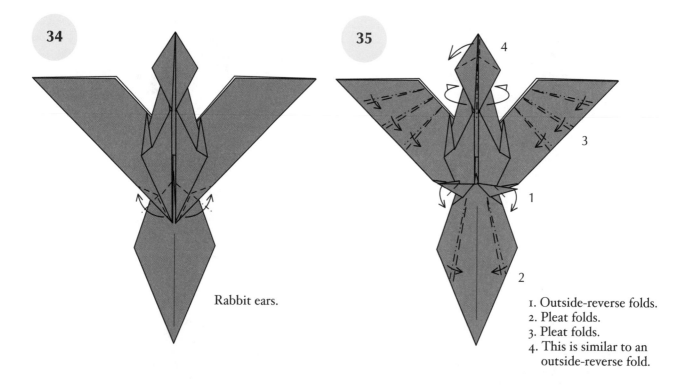

34

Rabbit ears.

35

1. Outside-reverse folds.
2. Pleat folds.
3. Pleat folds.
4. This is similar to an outside-reverse fold.

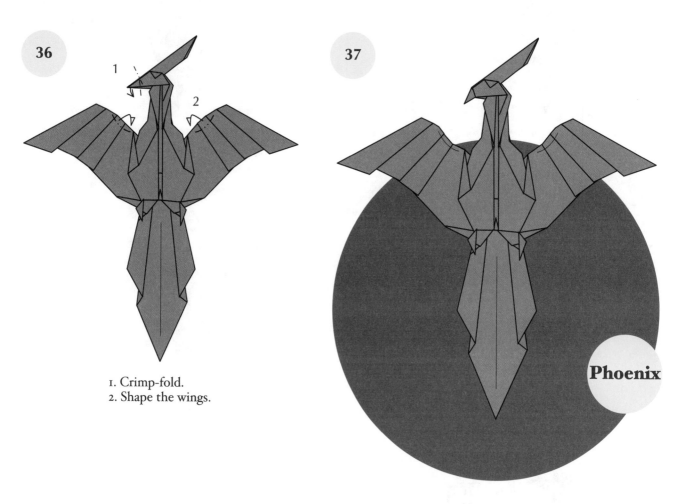

36

1. Crimp-fold.
2. Shape the wings.

37

Phoenix

Wyvern

With its two legs and long neck, Wyverns are ferocious fire-breathing creatures with a venomous bite. They can be found flying in pairs in search of dragons to feed upon. Humans usually would not interest them.

However, should they have a nest of young Wyverns, the flying pair would then search for the most accessible supply of food, to feed their brood. If spotted, you will quickly be carried away to their nest.

Be ready, be quick, and be prepared. Carry an origami Wyvern to show them. They will take the origami in their claws, and lie down for you to climb upon. They will fly you to their nest and their brood will sing to you. Be sure your folded Wyvern was done well, if the young ones do not approve, you will be their dinner.

1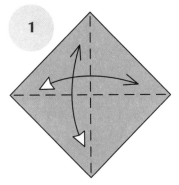

Fold and unfold.

2

Kite-fold and unfold.

3

Kite-fold and unfold.

4

Kite-fold and unfold.

5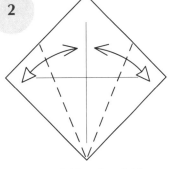

Fold and unfold.

6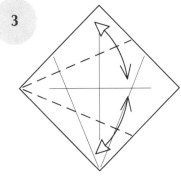

Fold and unfold.

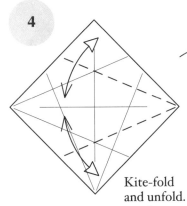

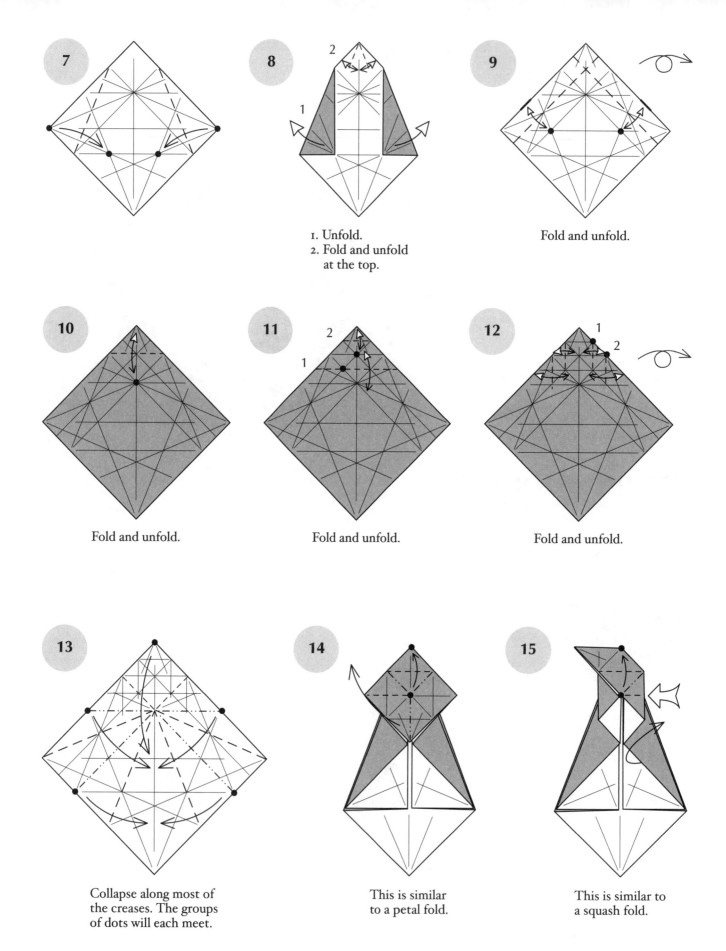

7

8
1. Unfold.
2. Fold and unfold
   at the top.

9
Fold and unfold.

10
Fold and unfold.

11
Fold and unfold.

12
Fold and unfold.

13
Collapse along most of
the creases. The groups
of dots will each meet.

14
This is similar
to a petal fold.

15
This is similar to
a squash fold.

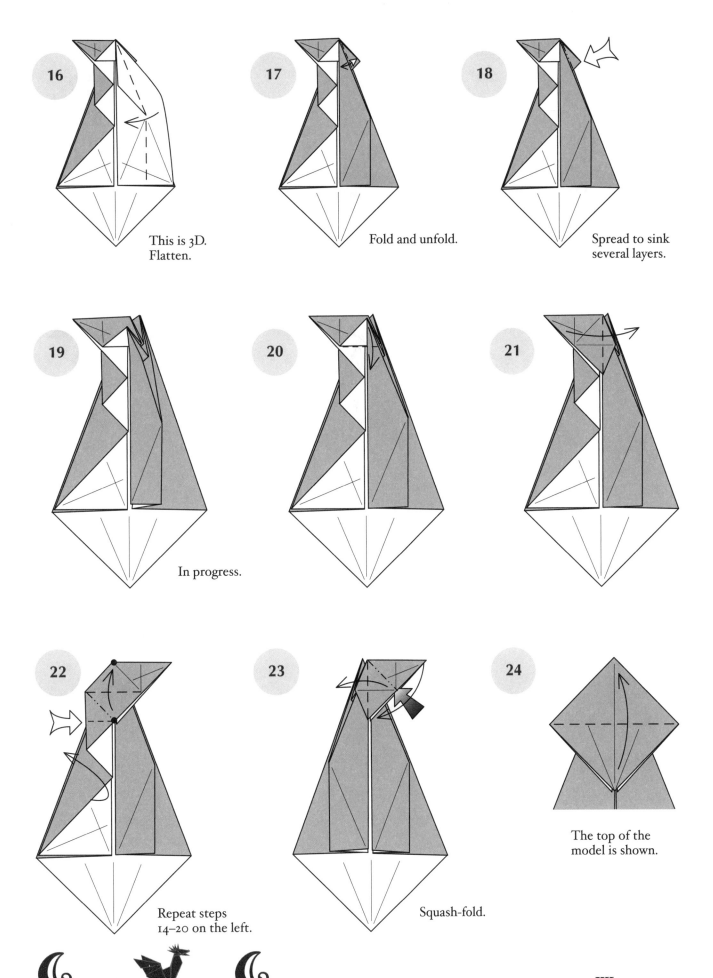

16 This is 3D. Flatten.

17 Fold and unfold.

18 Spread to sink several layers.

19 In progress.

20

21

22 Repeat steps 14–20 on the left.

23 Squash-fold.

24 The top of the model is shown.

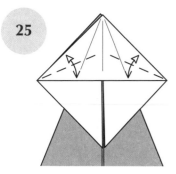

25

Fold and unfold
the top layer.

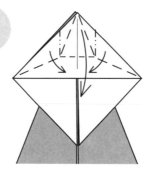

26

Fold along
the creases.

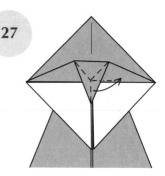

27

Rabbit-ear.

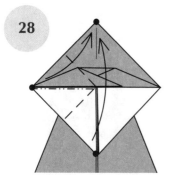

28

The dots will meet.

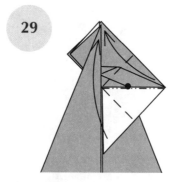

29

Keep the flap with
the dot on top.

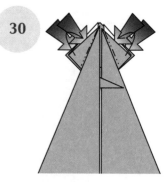

30

Four reverse folds.

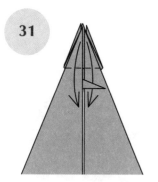

31

Fold four flaps.

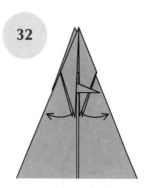

32

Slide the lower flaps.

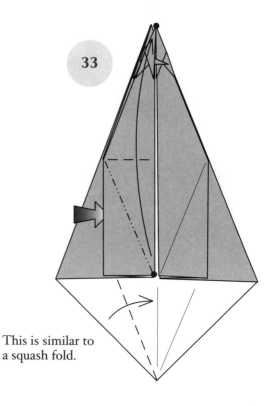

33

This is similar to
a squash fold.

34

This is 3D.
Flatten.

35

Repeat steps 33–34
on the right.

36

37

The dotted lines are
referred to in step 38.

38

Pull out the hidden layer,
same paper from step 37
in the dotted lines.

39

40

Wrap around.

41

Pull out
from inside.

42

Repeat steps 37–41
on the right.

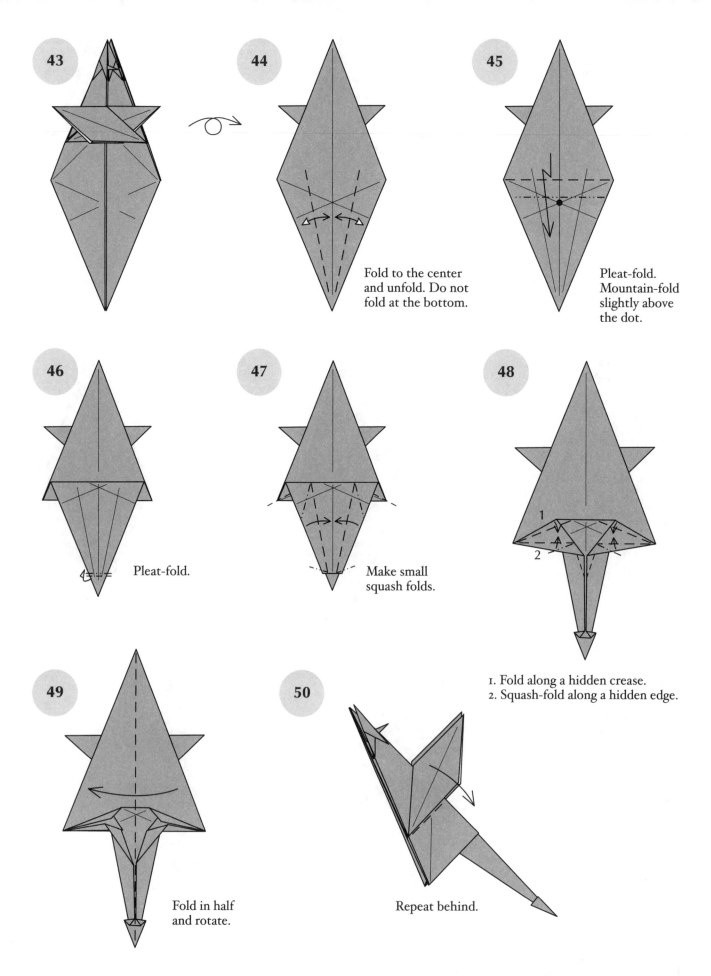

43

44

Fold to the center
and unfold. Do not
fold at the bottom.

45

Pleat-fold.
Mountain-fold
slightly above
the dot.

46

Pleat-fold.

47

Make small
squash folds.

48

1. Fold along a hidden crease.
2. Squash-fold along a hidden edge.

49

Fold in half
and rotate.

50

Repeat behind.

51

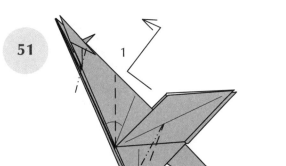

1. Outside-reverse folds.
2. Crimp-fold.

52

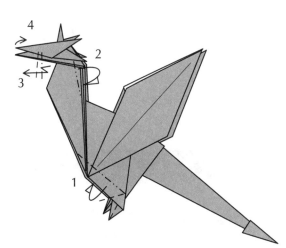

1. Shape the leg and body, repeat behind.
2. Fold two layers inside, repeat behind.
3. Crimp-fold.
4. Make a small outside-reverse fold and
   spread to form the nose.

53

Head detail.

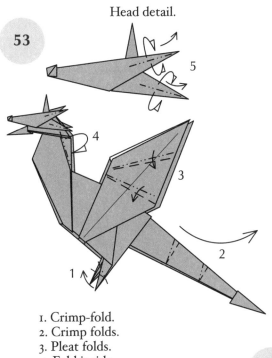

1. Crimp-fold.
2. Crimp folds.
3. Pleat folds.
4. Fold inside.
5. Thin the horns and
   slightly curl them.
Repeat behind.

54

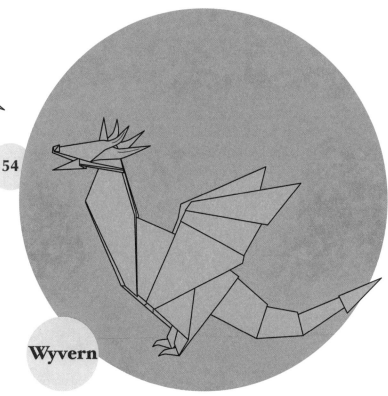

Wyvern

Winged Unicorn

The Winged Unicorn is the rarest of all the fantastic creatures. Should you find one, you must act immediately or you will never find one again. If you turn the pages without folding this, it will disappear forever.

Immediately fold this model, and a real Winged Unicorn will appear. You will have the healing power of the horn, making you invulnerable to dragons. All the creatures will treat you as the Enchanted King or Queen and offer you their finest foods, flights across the land, and gems. If you possess all the dragons and other fantastic creatures, you will at last become the Enchanted Master of Origami.

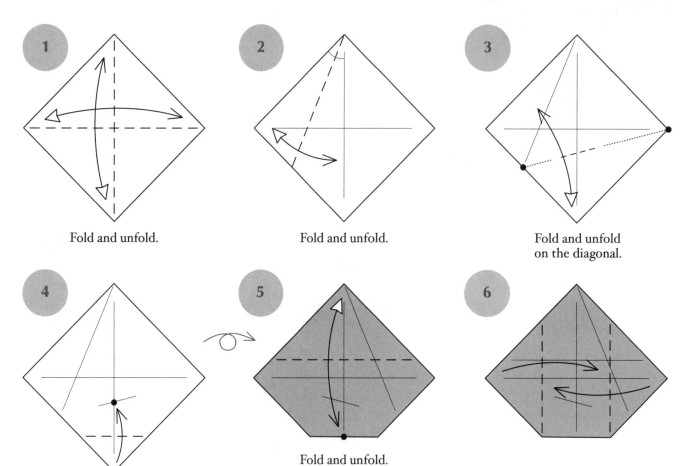

1 Fold and unfold.

2 Fold and unfold.

3 Fold and unfold on the diagonal.

4

5 Fold and unfold.

6

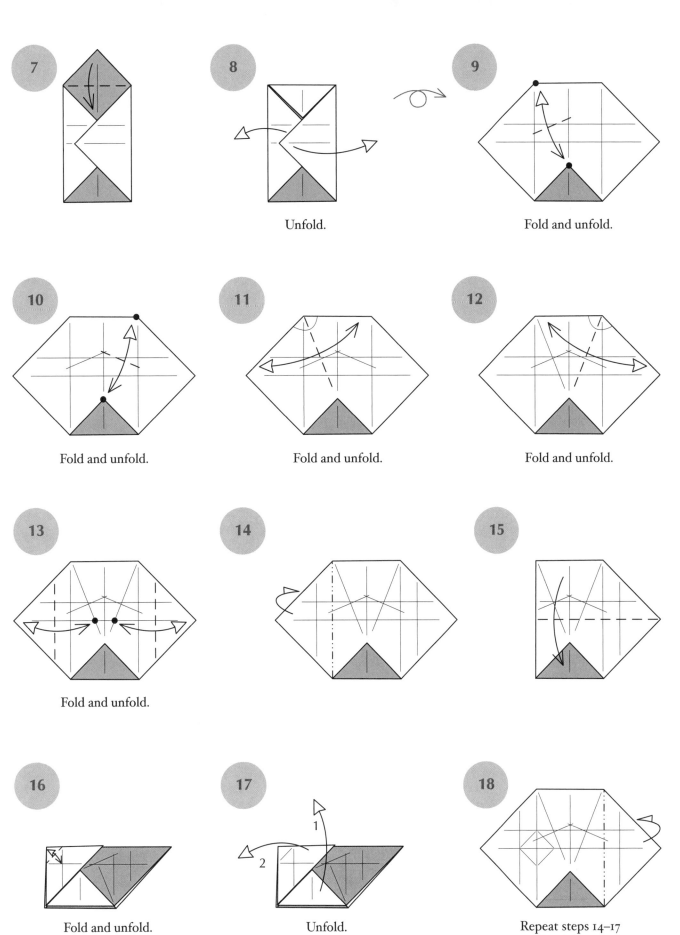

7

8

Unfold.

9

Fold and unfold.

10

Fold and unfold.

11

Fold and unfold.

12

Fold and unfold.

13

Fold and unfold.

14

15

16

Fold and unfold.

17

Unfold.

18

Repeat steps 14–17 on the right.

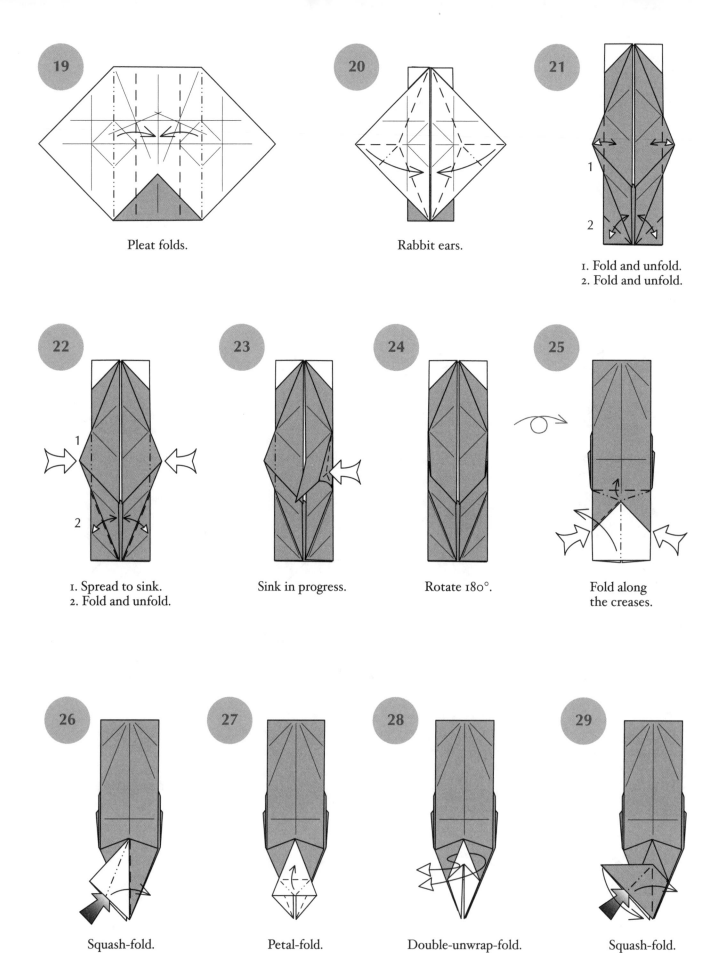

19 Pleat folds.

20 Rabbit ears.

21
1. Fold and unfold.
2. Fold and unfold.

22
1. Spread to sink.
2. Fold and unfold.

23 Sink in progress.

24 Rotate 180°.

25 Fold along the creases.

26 Squash-fold.

27 Petal-fold.

28 Double-unwrap-fold.

29 Squash-fold.

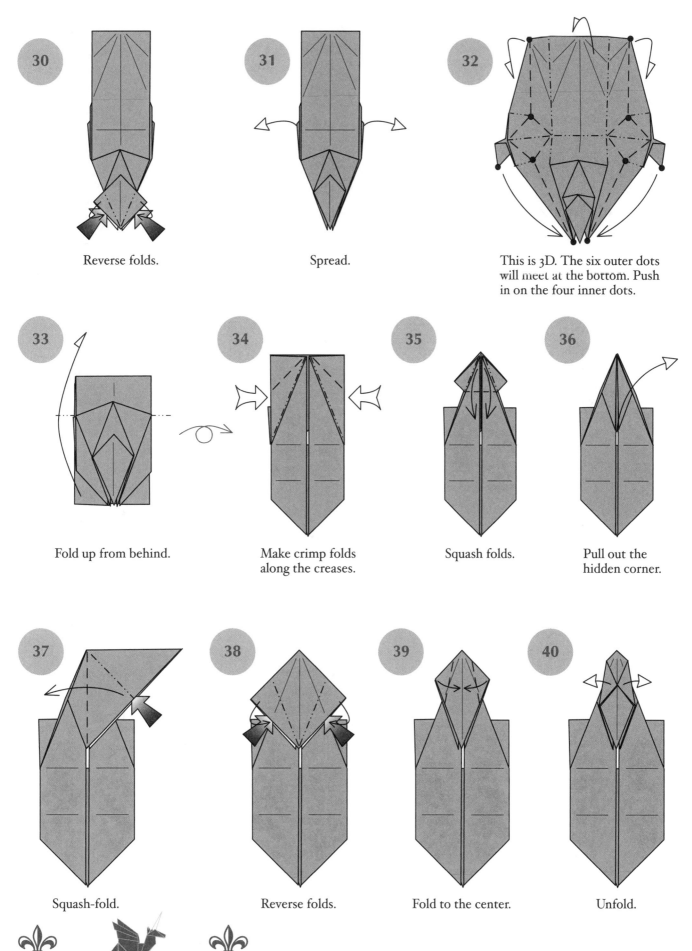

30 Reverse folds.

31 Spread.

32 This is 3D. The six outer dots will meet at the bottom. Push in on the four inner dots.

33 Fold up from behind.

34 Make crimp folds along the creases.

35 Squash folds.

36 Pull out the hidden corner.

37 Squash-fold.

38 Reverse folds.

39 Fold to the center.

40 Unfold.

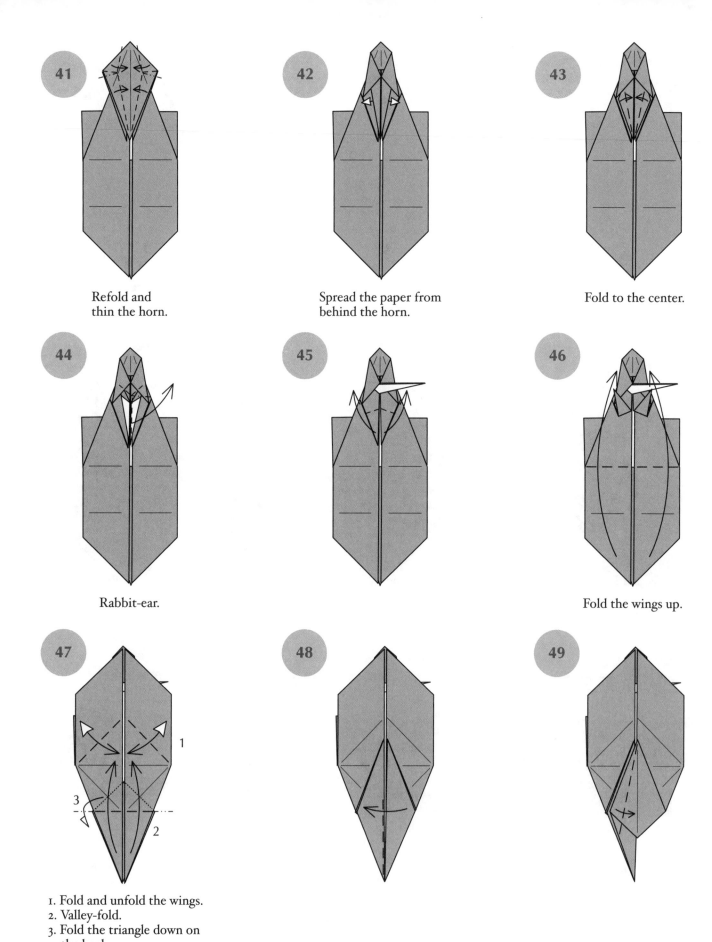

41 Refold and thin the horn.

42 Spread the paper from behind the horn.

43 Fold to the center.

44 Rabbit-ear.

45

46 Fold the wings up.

47
1. Fold and unfold the wings.
2. Valley-fold.
3. Fold the triangle down on the back.

48

49

50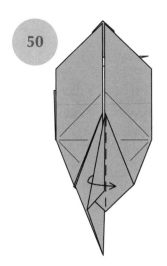

51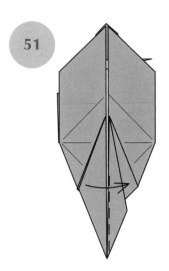

52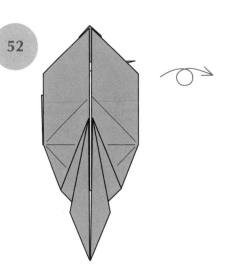

Repeat steps 48–50 in
the opposite direction.

53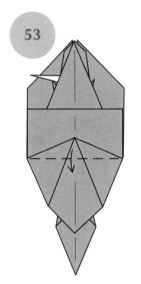

54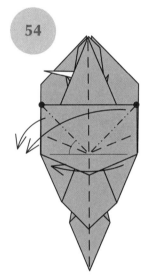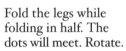

Fold the legs while
folding in half. The
dots will meet. Rotate.

55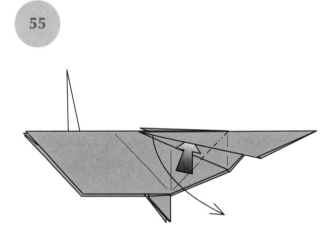

Reverse-fold, repeat behind.

56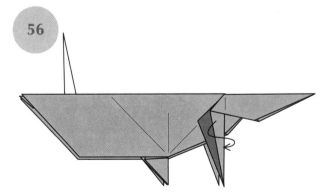

Tuck under the dark
paper. Repeat behind.

57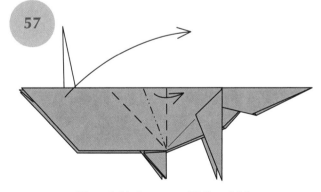

Pleat-fold the wings. Valley-fold
along the creases. Repeat behind.

Winged Unicorn 127

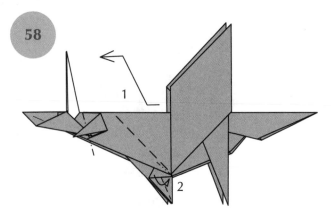

58

1. Outside-reverse folds. Fold along the crease at the valley line.
2. Reverse-fold, repeat behind.

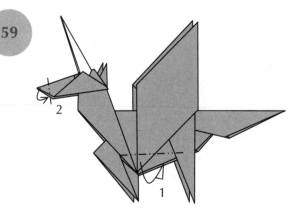

59

1. Fold the thick layers inside, repeat behind.
2. Reverse-fold.

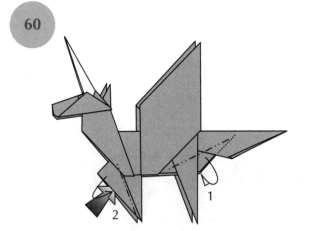

60

1. Fold inside, repeat behind.
2. Reverse-fold.

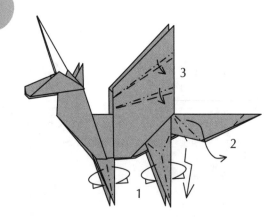

61

1. Thin and shape the legs.
2. Shape the tail with a crimp and outside-reverse fold.
3. Pleat the wings.
Repeat behind.

62

Winged Unicorn